POUNDS OR PINFOLDS AND LOCKUPS

ISBN 900843 34 9

Frontispiece: Bradwell-on-Sea, Essex

POUNDS OR PINFOLDS AND LOCKUPS

Beast and man in custody

B. M. WILLMOTT DOBBIE

Printed at the University of Bath

Bath University Library
1979

Figs 1 & 2 : Hope, Derbyshire. Before and after reconstruction

CONTENTS

Fig. 3 : Warwick

Fig. 4 : Near Poynings, Sussex

Fig. 5 : Bathford, Somerset.

Fig. 6 : Luckington, Wilts.

[Shows attempt to dislodge fastening]

[Rare example of hinged grille]

vi

PREFACE

It is strange that the many Pound Hills, Lanes, Streets, Farms, Cottages, Fields, and their relatives the Pinfolds, about the country excite neither remark nor interest, and though there are at least two hundred pounds and pinfolds in England surviving in good or fair condition, and many more in various stages of decay, few people will admit to having seen even one. Lockups, too, though familiar in the villages and towns to which they add a touch of interest, have mostly escaped curious notice.

If this study of these humble relics on the ground, and of the records which bring to life that multitude, man and beast, which has had close acquaintance with them, illuminates by a gleam our national past, or perhaps more important, encourages interest in their preservation, the labour of making it will have been worthwhile.

Ideally, I should have visited every example discovered, but this ambition has proved unattainable, usually because news was received after the recording tour of the district was made. Lockups were added at a late stage in the study when much of the country had already been visited. The volumes of Sir Nikolaus Pevsner's *The Buildings of England* have provided descriptions of lockups in several counties. These, and others which are not the writer's, are indicated in the Gazetteer.

I gladly thank the editors of the many periodicals: County Magazines, Women's Institute's Home and Country, The Local Council Review, The Village, The Ringing World, who published requests for information, and to the many readers who generously responded with so much local knowledge. I owe to them far more than could be particularly attributed in the text, and ask any who happen to read these words to accept this sincere acknowledgement. Friends, too, have been keen 'pound hounds', often going literally out of their way to 'bag' specimens, and have made valued additions to the score. I thank them, too.

Thanks are due to the many County Council officers who have answered enquiries, a few with comprehensive lists, most with goodwill but small contribution. Parish clerks have been especially helpful.

After all this, there must be many examples undiscovered. News of them will be gratefully received by the author.

Finally, I must express my special gratitude to Mr J. H. Lamble, Librarian, University of Bath, who has so kindly taken this little work into his personal care.

Fig. 7 : Ryton, Co. Durham

Fig. 8 : North Elmham, Norfolk

POUNDS AND PINFOLDS

INTRODUCTORY

A hundred years ago, the pound was a familiar feature of the village scene, the place of confinement of a diversity of creatures, as need arose. Within living memory, though much reduced in numbers, and decayed in function, it might still be a going concern. Today it is by comparison a rarity, too often falling into ruin, its purpose forgotten, the disreputable receptacle of litter and other noisome rubbish. It was the chance discovery of one such, a lasting blemish on the village scene, which first awakened interest in the writer and led to an absorbing chase through the counties of England.

As a reminder of a way of life so different from our own, as well as for the wealth of history belonging to it as an institution, the pound, where it survives, should be preserved. Fortunately, there is some evidence of increasing concern, and here and there the Parish Council or a local group is undertaking restoration; but many more examples await rescue, and rescue must be prompt.

The word pound is of Saxon origin: pund, an enclosure; and so is its near relative: pundfald, the modern pinfold. The south and west favour the former term, the north and east the latter. Birmingham has Pinfold Street in the city centre, and a notable pound at Northfield, a few miles to the south. In seventeenth century Warwickshire, in fact, the terms were employed indifferently. In this work pound is used, except where pinfold is used locally or occurs in a documentary source.

BY STATUTE ESTABLISHED

Sir Henry Maine, eminent among legal historians, wrote in 1875: 'There is no more ancient institution in our history than the village pound: it is far older than the King's Bench, and probably older than the Kingdom'.[1] He pointed out also that seizing another man's property (taking distress) in recompense for a debt, or in order to force payment, is such an obvious remedy that it was doubtless adopted early in the development of settled communities. 'The practice of Distress — of taking nams, a word preserved in the once famous law-term withernam — is attested by records considerably older than the Conquest. The examples of the right to distrain another man's property

1

which are most familiar to you are, I dare say, the landlord's right to seize the goods of his tenant for unpaid rent, and the right of the lawful possessor of land to take and impound stray beasts'.[2] Trespassing animals could be impounded 'damage feasant', that is, doing injury by breaking hedges, feeding, or even trampling the ground.

There are early references to pounds in the Bolden Buke,[3] a survey of the manors of the See of Durham made in 1183, and in a perambulation of Chute Forest (Wiltshire) during the reign of Henry 2 (died 1189): 'From that same house to the house of William le Bond which is called Pundfald'.[4]

Much legislation, ancient and modern, deals with the taking of distress: a dangerous swamp for amateur dabbling, so only dealt with in outline here. The Statute of Marlborough (1267)[5] lays down that no man shall take satisfaction on his own account, but only through the King's court; that is, he may seize property and impound it, but must then submit to legal judgement. He may not drive any distress out of the county where it was taken, nor take unreasonable distress. He may not take distresses out of his fee (the estate to which he belongs), nor in the King's highway, nor in the common street.

Three important enactments were made in the Statutes of the Exchequer[6], the date of which is uncertain, but which probably followed soon after the Statute of Marlborough. The first is that a man whose beasts are impounded for a distress has the right to feed them and they may not be sold within fifteen days; the second, that the beasts that work a man's land may not be seized; and the third that the value of the distress seized shall be reasonable in relation to the value of the debt, and be estimated by neighbours, not by strangers.

The Statute of Marlborough is in Latin, the Statutes of the Exchequer in Norman French. The Distress Act of 1554[7] is in English, and the actual wording is revealing:

'For thavoiding of grevous vexations exactions troubles and disorder in taking of distresses and impoundyng of cattayle: Be it enacted by thaucthorite of the presente Parliament that . . . no distress of cattell shall bee dryven out of the hundred rape wapentake or lathe where such ys or shalbe taken, excepte it bee to a pownde overte within the said shyre, nor above three myles distante from the place where the said distresse ys taken; and that no cattell or other goodes, distreigned or taken by way of distresse for any maner of cause at one tyme, shalbe impounded in severall places, whereby the owner or owners of such distress shall be constreyned to sue several replevis for the delyverye of the said distresse so taken at one tyme; upon payne every persone offending contraye to this Acte shall forfaite to the partye greved for every suche offence, one hundred shillings and treble damages.

'And . . . that . . . no person or persons shall take for keping impounde impownding or pondage of any maner of distres, above the some of 4d for any one hole distres that shalbe so impounded, and where les hathe bene used, ther to take les, upon the payne of fyve powndes to be payd to the partis greved, over and besides suche monye as he shall take above the some of 4d any usage or prescription to the contrary in any wise notwithstanding'.

By replevin the seized goods were returned to their owner on a pledge to submit to the decision of a court of justice. A hundred shillings seems an enormous fine, especially compared with the maximum fee of fourpence allowed to the keeper of the pound for a whole distress. The hundred is a subdivision of a shire, and was administered by a King's court, presided over by the Sheriff or his deputy. A local landowner might rank as lord of the hundred. A large structure which survives at Gwithian (Cornwall) is believed to be the pound of the hundred of Penwith.[8] Elsewhere, hundred pounds seem to have disappeared.

It is worthy of note that a distress was expected usually to be livestock. This was doubtless because by far the most valuable of a man's property was likely to be his beasts, as appears very clearly in inventories.

THE PINDER

In feudal times the custodian of the pound was an official of the manor, appointed and sworn at the court leet, and responsible to the lord. Generally, his title was pinder; in a few places, Hutton-le-Hole (Yorkshire) is an example, the pinder is still appointed. The pinder of Wakefield is commemorated in a song:

> In Wakefield there lives a jolly Pinder,
> In Wakefield all on a green . . . *

Hope (Derbyshire) still has its pound keeper in active service. Canterbury had its pound keeper; at Rochester the office was beadle and poundkeeper, evidently controlled by the borough. The boroughs of Pevensey and Winchelsea (Sussex) had pound drivers, and Walton on the Hill (Staffordshire) appointed its penner at least as late as 1910. Alnwick had a keeper of the pinfold.

The office is, as it were, fossilised in surnames such as Pinder, Pounder, Poynder, Ponder, and also Pinfold, Penfold and Pinfield. The borough of Berwick on Tweed had its fieldgrieves, who evidently also looked after the common fields. It was not unusual for the hayward, whose main task was the regulation of the fields and commons, to be also in charge of the pound. This was so at Batheaston (Somerset) and at Langton Matravers (Dorset), where the hayward had his cottage close by the pound. At Peterborough a sixteenth century entry in the manor court roll records this admonition:

Y Hayward, Beadle or Greve, his oath.

You shall swear that you shall well and truly serve the office of a Hayward, Beadle or Greve for the year to come. You shall duly and truly Execute all such processes as shall be directed unto you from this Court, and you shall from time to time present and certify all such Pound breaches and rescues as shall happen to be made within your office, and likewise you shall present all such cattle Estreyed as shall usually come within your said office. And in everything, you shall well and truly behave yourself in your said office during the terme aforesaid. So help you God.[9]

A solemn warning indeed

The officer responsible for the pound could expect some recompense for his pains, and it took a variety of forms. The Bolden Buke[10] includes an early record of the payment received by the 'punderus' (translated pounder) of the various manors of the See of Durham in the twelfth century. The editor says: 'The pounder was an officer of the lord, and in Bolden Buke we find him receiving remuneration in the shape of land from the Bishop for his service, and also a further payment in kind from the tenants, who gave him so many thraves (sheaves) of corn from each plough of their village. With this corn he probably provided the cattle in his custody with food, receiving payment for it from the owners. His return to the lord consisted, in the Palatinate, of hens and eggs, of which he rendered a very large number'.

The fine pinfold at Ryton (Fig. 7) (probably not the original structure), in the See of Durham was restored in 1974, and there the Bolden Buke records that the pounder had five acres, and thraves of corn like the other pounders, and rendered to the lord, in this case the Bishop, 30 hens and 200 eggs. Of the same manor of Ryton, Bishop Hatfield's survey[11] of about 1380 records:

OFFICIUM PUNDERI. Robertus Newcomen ten. terras voc. Punderlond, cont. v acr. terrae, et habet de tenentibus sicut alii de consuetudine officii, et red. ad festum Natalis Domini et ad festum Paschae xxx gallinas et ccxl ova.

DUTY OF THE POUNDER. Robert Newcomen holds the lands called Punderland, containing 5 acres, and has from the tenants the same as the others of similar office, and renders at Christmas and Easter 30 hens and 240 eggs.

No other instance has been noticed of the keeper of the pound paying a fee for the office. As for his remuneration, though the Distress Act of 1554 lays down that no more than four pence is to be taken for one whole distress, in practice the penalty seems to have been a matter of local custom. For instance: 'One manor laid down in 1789 . . . for every score of sheep 2d, a sow and pigs 4d, horse or beast 1d. At Christmas every farmer 2d and every cottager 1d apiece. Penalty for not paying pindar's fees 6d'[12] Anyone who has attempted to persuade pigs will agree with the seemingly generous payment.

4

At Hope (Derbyshire), where the pinfold is still in use (Fig. 1), the pinder has a small payment for each animal impounded, and the use of the Pinner's Meadow, a charity administered by trustees.[13]

RESCUE

If the owner of goods or cattle distrained offered full recompense or denied the charge, he was not committing an offence if he rescued his property, though if he were subsequently found guilty he would suffer. Here is an early example of rescue:

> 1271 Philippus le Balismit in misericordia eo quod denegavit Johannem Budell volentem parcare averia sua.

> 1271 Philip le Balismit in mercy because he resisted John the Bailiff when he wanted to put his animals in the pound.[14]

The rescue, however, must be before the chattels reach the pound. Once impounded, they are *in custodia legis* and can only be released following a legal process. Other examples of rescue are:

> 1631 John Heminge, for rescuing six sheep being brought towards the common pound for trespassing in the fields at Haselor.[15]

> 1640 Agnes Chamberlayne and Thomas Wyse of Monckeskerby fined for rescuing a cow of one John Robertes, being taken for a distress.[15]

> 1658 Walter Devereux of Astley, gentleman, indicted for assaulting Thomas Sprigge and John Bayly, having distrained thirty sheep of the said Walter's for rent due to the said Thomas, and for rescous of the distress.[15]

> 1647 Philippe Doale and his two sonnes John and Henry rescued theire sheepe from our sworne Hayward and John Hampton.[16]

Cattle may lawfully be impounded in a private pound, but they are not then *in custodia legis*, and the impounder must release them if satisfaction is offered. Thomas Hurdys was not acting unlawfully:

> 1635 Nicholas Latham of Atherston upon Stower, shepherd, indicted for unlawfully taking away four heifers out of the yard of one Thomas Hurdys, they being there impounded for a trespass done in the close of the said Hurdys.[17]

An impounder in a private pound must give notice to the owner to feed his animals. If he puts them in a closed place or building he must feed them at his own expense. Impounded cattle may only be worked for their own benefit, such as the milking of cows.

POUNDBREACH

When cattle have been impounded in the common pound and are therefore lawfully in custody it is a misdemeanour, punishable by fine, imprisonment, or both, to break into the pound in order to release them. As might be expected, many such misdemeanours are to be found in court records, of which the following are representative:

1298 Et Nigellus venit. Et dicit quod ipse habuit in precepto ad leuandum 36s de debito domini regis pro quo quidem debito ipse cepit sex iumenta nomine districcionis et ea imparcauit. Et quia predictus Walterus parcem contra pacem domini regis fregit et predicta abduxit. Attachiauit dictum Walterum ad respondendum coram vicecomite.[18]

1298 And Nigel has come, and says that he had in command to levy 36s in respect of a debt of the lord king, for which debt he took six mares in the name of distraint and impounded them. And because the aforesaid Walter did break the pound against the lord king's peace and the aforesaid mares did carry away, he attached the said Walter to answer before the sheriff.

1462 12d fine for breaking the pinfold.[19]

1586 Jas. (Jacobus) Whythhurst for breaking the pound at Overteyne, and taking a heifer which Ric. Phillips constable of Overteyne and Netherteyne had distrained for 21d due for tenths and fifteenths.[20]

1589 Item we present harie milles hathe made pound breache for that he coused 4 hogges to be lyfted over the pound by som one and other wherefore he hath forfeited according to the statute £5.[21]

1601 Thomas phillpott by his servaunts broke the pounde and locke and took out 5 or 6 hogges.[22]

1611 That Whereas George James did wilfullye and stubbornelye Resyste the orders and decrees made for the benefitt and good of the inhabitants of the Borrow of Calne in Breakinge the pounde. That he submitt hymself for his ffollye cravinge the Burgessz ffavoure herein. And pmysinge to mend up the pounde agayne and to make it good as it was before. And that he gave in Recompense to the towene xiid.[23]

1681 Netheravon petition to the Dean of Sarum against the Vicar: 'He trespassed with his horse or geldinge which being impounded for damage feasant he broak the pound and tooke him away contrary to lawe'.[24]

1736 James Ellis of Marston in Potterne, tailor, for breaking the pound at Marston and leading away his grey mare, which had been impounded for damage done by it in the clover field of Marston. Indictment found.[25]

Under the Distress for Rent Act 1689, 'upon any pound breach or rescous of goods or chattells distrained for rent the person or persons grieved thereby shall in a speciall action upon the case for the wrong thereby sustained recover his and their treble damages . . . against the offender or offenders in any such rescous or pound-breach any or either of them or against the owners of the goods distrained in case the same be afterwards found to have come to his use or possession'. The risk of treble damages might seem a fairly strong deterrent, and was perhaps effective. However, the Pound-Breach Act of 1843 put a limit of five pounds on the fine to be ordered on conviction for pound breach. Amended by the Criminal Justice Act 1967, rescue without lawful authority or excuse and pound breach are each liable to a penalty of twenty pounds. A conviction under this Act would indeed be 'news'! The latest conviction for poundbreach noted by the writer was at Coleford in 1929. (P16).

Payment for watching the pounds seems an obvious device to prevent poundbreach, though such a transaction does not commonly appear in records. The following instances were noticed:

1647 For watching the pound when Thomas sheepe were impounded for not payeing his dewes 6d.

1651 Watching the Marsh pound and taking the thief 4s.[26]

PROVISION, OWNERSHIP AND MAINTENANCE

At least by the time the feudal system was fully established, the pound was a manorial institution, under the authority of the lord, and regulated by the manorial court. In illustration of the unplanned way in which the system grew up: when the Quo Warranto proceedings of the late thirteenth and the fourteenth centuries investigated the jurisdictions of lords of manors, few could shew any document giving the right to hold courts.[27] So it is not surprising that the practices known as 'the custom of the manor' varied from place to place. In general, it was the acknowledged duty of the lord to provide and maintain a pound. There is an early example in the reeve's draft account for Severhampton (Wiltshire) in 1275/6[28]:

In muro faciendo circa pondfoldam de 8 perticiis 3s.

For making the wall round the pound of 8 perches 3s.

The manor court rolls of Swindon[29] for 1645 record that the homage (tenants) complains that 'there is no collistringus, Angl. Pillory, abacus, Angli Cuckingstole, nec cippi, Angli stocks, within the borough of Swindon', and adds the lack of a 'parcus, Angli Pound', and the jurymen declare that 'Richard Goddard, Lord of the Manor, ought to see to this, and because of this, is in mercy', that is, liable to a penalty.

Full equipment would entail pound, stocks, lockup, pillory, whipping

7

post, cucking or ducking stool, but the last three are rarely mentioned in court rolls, and few of them survive. Malvern (Worcestershire) still has its pound, stocks and whipping post in association, and Coleshill (Warwickshire) retains its whipping post and pillory. There is a ducking stool in the Church of Leominster.

The following examples are illustrative. The manor roll of Grittleton (Wiltshire)[30] in 1632 records that the lady of the manor is responsible for the repair of the pound, but she had attempted to infringe the ancient customs of the manor. After many protests made by the homage the dispute was carried before a higher court, the tenants won their case, and the ancient Customs of the Manor, already written, were declared to be legally binding upon the lady of the manor as well as her tenants.

> 1663 John Hunt of Haverhill, Co. Essex, gentleman, lord of the manor and parish of Baldock, has not erected a pound for the benefit of the manor and parish of Baldock, and he ought to erect and repair it whenever necessary.

In this case, the dispute was taken to the Quarter Sessions.[31] The lord of the manor of Taunton was in trouble in 1583 for neglecting to repair the pound, and in 1638 John Mallett, lord of the sub-manor of Lydeard Punchardon in the same jurisdiction was fined for neglecting to repair his pound.[32]

Nevertheless, the duty was liable to be imposed on the homage:

> 1420 26 Sep Concordatum est hic in curia inter tenentes ville de Islep' videlicet quod ipsi tenentes bene et competenter facient et emendabunt parcum suum citra festum Pasche proximum futurum sub pena 6s 8d[33]

> 1420 26 Sep It it is agreed here in court among the tenants of the vill of Islip that they shall rightly and competently make and repair their pound before the feast of Easter next to come, pain of 6s 8d.

> 1592 Willelmus Howyt et Johannes Coke quia non reparaverunt partes suas, Anglice theyr partis of the Pound, ideo ipsi sunt separatim in misericordiam 12d.[34]

> 1592 William Howyt and John Coke because they had not repaired their parts of the Pound, therefore they are each in mercy 12d.

> 1612 We present that the pounde wall is in decaye and is to be repayred by the tennents, the walles by the coppeholders and the dore by the farmer to be amended.[35]

The instances quoted above point to three differing customs in three manors regarding repair of the pound.

There is an interesting sequence in the Warwick Quarter Sessions Records:[36]

> 1642 The inhabitants of Little Packington presented for default of having no pinfold there. Fined.

1649 William Baldwin of Henley, gentleman, indicted for not repairing the common pound there.
Ralph Price of Spernall indicted for not repairing the pinfold, being constable.
1652 Bascot inhabitants presented for not repairing of the common pound there. Fined.

The terms pound and pinfold were evidently used indifferently in Warwickshire at this time. What is more important is that by the seventeenth century the King's courts of Quarter Sessions were replacing the manorial courts. The observation raises a subject germane to this study: the decay and virtual extinction of that essentially mediaeval institution, the manor, with its intricate system of rights and duties between lords and tenants. Feudalism died a slow death: as late as the reign of Elizabeth a fugitive from his manor could not be quite certain that he would not be pursued and brought back. Even today, the title Lord of the Manor persists and is a marketable commodity, and manorial courts are still held here and there.

A recent (1976) report of the Law Commission on the Jurisdiction of Certain Ancient Courts recommended that where a jurisdiction is not obsolete, and both lord and court wish it to continue, it should remain in being. The business transacted is usually the regulation of commons, and 'the taking of presentments with respect to matters of local concern'. Among surviving courts which have in their control a pound or pinfold are: Spaunton (Hutton-le-Hole) and Mickley (both Yorkshire), Laxton (Notting-hamshire), Bucklebury (Berkshire), Spitchwick (Devonshire), Portland, Southampton (Fig. 9); Langton Matravers, Watchet (site) and Wareham, (all Dorset), and the Verderers' Courts of Dean Forest and New Forest.

The Cottingham and Middleton (Market Harborough) copyholders bought their pounds from the lord of the manor about 1614, and still own them. Elsewhere, in recent times the lord of the manor has disposed of the pounds. Lord Braybrooke presented that of Waltham S. Lawrence (Berkshire)(Fig. 14) to the village in 1937, and sold the pound of Saffron Walden (Essex) to the Borough Council for £5 in 1958. The pound of West Bradford (Lancashire) was given to the parish by Lord Clitheroe, and so was that of Rippingale (Lincolnshire) by the lord of the manor. The pound at Beckley (Oxfordshire) was sold to a private owner by the Duke of Abingdon within recent years.

From quite early days towns, especially incorporated ones, provided them-selves with the necessary convenience of a pound. In the records of the Borough of Henley[37], for example, appears:

1424 Item soulut (sic) [paid] pur une cartfulle tenet for a pownde for hoggis xiid. Item for makyng of the hedge iid Item for a dore vid Item with twestys et staples viid.
Item solut Rob. Boys pro una placea terre [piece of ground] for ye pounde per annum xvid.

9

The Guild Stewards' Book of Calne (Wiltshire)[38] preserves many entries relating to the two pounds serving the commons controlled by the borough. Local government was often identified with the authority of a merchant guild as a stage in the development of a municipality. In Calne, also, the hundred pound survived into the twentieth century.

As feudalism was so long in dying, the intervention of the Vestry, representing the parish, was a gradual process, rarely recorded as such. Generally, entries relating to the pound, such as the cost of repairs or the offence of poundbreach, begin to appear in the churchwardens' or overseers' accounts; where the constable kept accounts entries may be found therein, such as those of Doveridge (Derbyshire):

1720 pd for gravelling the poundfould 3s 4d.[39]

The stage of transition is illustrated also in the case of Somerton (Somerset), an ancient borough: 'By the mid seventeenth century there were two constables, one for the manor, and one for the borough, but both answerable to the borough court ... Abandonment of manorial courts after 1863 left the Vestry the sole governing body of the town'.[40]

Bishop Hobhouse[41] summarises the process thus: 'On the Vestry succeeding the Hundred and Manor Courts the care of the Pound, the appointment of Hayward, the repair of Stocks, and appointment of tythingmen often lapsed into its hands'. He might have added constables.

There is a modern example of collaboration at Follifoot (Yorkshire), where the pound belongs to the lord of the manor, is kept in repair by the parish, and was thoroughly restored with the aid of public subscription in 1975.

Parishes have sold their pounds, especially of late years, so that the seeker may have much difficulty in determining ownership. The usual answer today is 'the Council', but the Council conveniently to itself may deny responsibility! A solitary instance was found at West Wratting (Cambridgeshire) of a pound owned by the Church. A notice on the gate reads 'Church Property'.

SITE AND STRUCTURE

There seems to be little significance in the siting of the pound. There is plenty of evidence of the moving of pounds, and the structure that we see is unlikely to be more than two or at most three centuries old, often much less. Though the lord was the owner, and had an interest in what went on, few have been noted in the vicinity of the Home Farm or Manor House: Threshfield and Hutton Ambo (both Yorkshire). Anywhere in the village street is the place to look, near or on the Green, or close beside the Church. A pound near the common is obviously a convenience, Wimbledon and Hampstead Heath being examples in London, carefully preserved. A crossroads is also a likely site. The seeker should not lose heart when a number of enquiries finds no answer. Perseverance usually discovers an old resident who knows.

A few parishes have two pounds: Epworth (Lincolnshire), Long Compton (Warwickshire), probably denoting the previous existence of two manors. This was certainly the case at Barston (Warwickshire). The occasional siting of a pound far from any settlement or a common suggests a manor which has disappeared.

There are places where the present pound is a small field, or nothing more than a lightly fenced area, quite unsuitable for anything but the convenient securing of strays out of harm's way. This is probably a comparatively modern arrangement. At Corfe Castle (Dorset), where a small paddock is known as the pound, an excellent stone built structure stands within a few yards. It may be remarked here that in local lore a lockup is sometimes confused with a pound.

The Commons Registration Act of 1965 resulted in the registration as common or village green of many pounds and pound sites; the county lists are a useful source of information. The question whether a pound may lawfully be classed as common land was decided in the affirmative in an enquiry held by the Commons Commissioners with regard to the land known as Pinfold, Higham (Lancashire). That pinfold was derelict in 1975. Some registrations under the Act pose a problem, for example, a triangular patch of ground at a road junction, with no relic whatever of a structure, no bricks, stones or bits of old fencing. This is strange, and suggests that such sites are secondary, and perhaps were used for tethering strays. An unfenced bit of ground at Ryton (Shropshire) is known as the Donkey Pound. At Rous Lench (Worcestershire) and Alconbury Weston (Huntingdonshire) a strip of roadside verge is called 'the pound'. Such sites cannot date from the time when the pound was a secure enclosure, and conviction for poundbreach still a reality.

Many pounds are four-sided, square, rectangular, or irregular, according to the shape of the plot of ground conveniently available. Others are circular, especially in Yorkshire, Derbyshire and Suffolk. The pounds of Anstey (Leicestershire) (Fig. 10) and Waterfall (Derbyshire) are horseshoe shaped. Raskelf (Yorkshire) (Fig. 16) pinfold is unique: quite 'Gothick', octagonal, ten feet in height, castellated, with a barred window on either side of the doorway. A remarkable pound is to be seen at Wolverley (Worcestershire): an enclosure hollowed out of a sandstone outcrop, with three round-headed deep recesses fashioned in the back wall. They must have been contrived for some purpose other than the confinement of animals, perhaps to contain impounded goods, which were required to be kept in a covered pound.

In stone country of course the natural material was used, in various styles,

11

drystone or rubble, often roughly coursed. Dressed stone might be used, with an elegant effect: examples are at Barlow (Derbyshire), Berkswell (Warwickshire) and Capenhurst (Cheshire). Wilmington and Slindon (Sussex) have flint pounds, and the one at Gimingham (Norfolk) is of flint and brick. Elsewhere, pounds are generally of brick. Many examples, both in stone and in brick, carry a neat coping. A few are constructed with iron railings: Wymeswold (Leicestershire), Fingest (Buckinghamshire), Lambourne End (Essex).

There must have been timber-built pounds in plenty, especially in non-stone country, but most have decayed and disappeared, or survive as a few pathetic lengths of rotten wood. There is a fine pound at Park Pike in the Forest of Dean. (Fig. 11). It has two compartments and covered mangers, and is occasionally used. The timber pound at Feckenham (Worcestershire) is well looked after, and has been restored within fairly recent time. The wooden pounds at Woburn (Bedfordshire) and Speen (Berkshire) badly need attention (1975). Wooden pounds are usually of the post-and-rail variety, with the lower half subdivided to restrain small animals. The pound in which Mr Pickwick was confined is a good example, but the source of the artist's inspiration has defied discovery.

The height of walls is of some interest. Five feet or so must be sufficient to confine all prisoners but the most active horses, who might be expected to achieve such a leap. A greater height must have been intended to thwart attempts at poundbreach — eight or nine feet is not unusual — and suggests a structure of some antiquity. Heights exceeding five feet are usually indicated in the gazetteer. Much lower walls are frequent, and must have presented only a minor obstacle to large animals, and little hindrance to release.

A few pounds have convenient equipment for the inmates: a stream, North Stoke (Somerset), Spennithorne (Yorkshire); a trough, Lower Bebington (Cheshire). Tunbridge Wells (Fig. 15) and Park Pike (Forest of Dean) (Fig. 11) have covered mangers.

SUNDRY PENALTIES

In early days, fines were imposed by the manorial court. The court roll of Castle Combe (Wiltshire)[42] records in the year 1674 that when trespassing cattle are impounded twopence for each beast goes to the pinder and the same to the lord.

When the parish took over, probably custom ruled. More formal provision might be made. Under an Act of 1814 for lighting, watching and improving the town of Dartford, the Commissioners were entitled to make a charge of five shillings for each animal impounded, together with a reasonable charge for expenses and keep of animals so impounded and, 'if such charges and expenses be not paid within five days such animals should be sold and the balance, after such fine of five shillings and expenses, be paid to the owner of such impounded animals'.[43]

The pound of Hope (Derbyshire) (Fig. 1), is probably the only remaining village pound for which fines are still levied. The charge for keeping is 3d a day for sheep. 1s 6d for cattle. After notification of the owner, animals are kept for three weeks, and then sold at market, one a week, to pay for food. The pinner receives a small payment for every animal impounded.[44]

LATER LEGISLATION SUMMARISED

Legislation to quite recent times witnesses to the continuing, though in practice much diminished, possibility of impounding.

The person taking an animal to the pound, not the pound keeper, is responsible for feeding and watering it. He may, of course, recover the cost from the owner. If any impounded animal is without sufficient food or water for six successive hours, any person may enter the pound to supply it, and recover the cost as a civil debt.

Cattle straying on the highway, except where it crosses a common, may be impounded.

The maximum penalty for poundbreach was in 1967 increased from £5 to £20.

The offence of damage feasant was abolished by the Animals Act of 1971. Henceforth the person aggrieved must sue for damages in the civil court.

While distraint and impounding are still legal, the remaining functions of the pound in practice are thus summarised in Halsbury's Laws of England, 4th edition, 1971:

Now that the right of distress damage feasant has been abolished, the only remaining relevance of pounds would seem to be in connection with distress for rent or after removal of any animal from the highway under the Highways Act 1959.

Obviously, our pounds and pinfolds are unlikely to be again in brisk business, but it is interesting to be reminded that they may still lawfully be used. The past lingers into the present.

THE POUND IN DEFENCE OF COMMON RIGHTS

Commoners are naturally jealous of their customary rights, and impounding of animals found illegally pasturing is an obvious device, especially where the common is stinted. Examples are not hard to come by:

From the records of Southampton Court Leet.[45]

> 1550 And yf eny that be or shalbe put in truste to oversee the comyn as aforesaid, shall overcharge the comyn, he shall forfeyt for every Defaulte 3s 4d, and who that findeth yt and puttith theire Cattall in pounde shall have halffe for his laboure.

> 1566 Ffyrste yt is agreed that the drevers shall evere 14 dayes at the least Vew the comyns abowte the towne to see yf eny do surcharge the same, as yf eny townes man have above the numbere of two beasse or that there be eny strang beasse theere and yf there be to bring them to the pounde and the drivers to take for evere beaste soo takne and pounded 4d.

From a deed executed by the commoners of Batheaston (Somerset) in 1719 and preserved in the parish:

> Item . . . that all Sheep Horses and Cattle that shall at any time be found in the said Commons or Common feilds contrary to this Agreement . . shall be sent to the Common Pound and there remain till satisfaction made. For every Sheep Two Shillings and Sixpence and for every Horse or Beast Five Shillings for every Days voluntary Trespass.

> Item . . . as a further encouragement to the Hayward to be dilligent in the execution of his Office . . . he shall be entitled to Twelvepence for every time that any Horses Beasts or Sheep shall be actually impounded for trespassing in the Common Fields . . . And tis also agreed that all and every Horse Beast and Sheep that shall be found so trespassing shall by the Hayward . . . be sent to and detained in the Common Pound untill such payment be made over and above satisfaction for the trespass.

How far such rules had the force of law may be questioned, but there is no doubt of the severity of the penalties.

FOREST POUNDS

Special functions attach to forest pounds. Under Forest Law provision was made for 'drifts of the forest' to be made at least once a year, when all the stock was rounded up and driven to the pounds. An Act of 1541 ordered driving yearly 'at the Feast of S. Michael the Archangel' or within fifteen days after. The purpose of the drifts was summarised in 1648 by the jurist, Edward Coke: [46]

> All the cattle as well of commoners as of strangers are driven by the officers of the forest to some certain pound or place enclosed, and the end thereof is threefold, viz. First to see whether those that ought to common do common with such kind of cattle as by prescription or grant they ought, Secondly, if they have common with such cattle as they ought, whether they do surcharge or no. Thirdly, if the cattle of any stranger be there which ought not to common at all.

Common rights are a very ancient institution, antedating the Royal Forests made by the Norman Kings, and continued with the ruthless Forest Law superimposed. Even the Conqueror could not abolish common rights, a mercy for which the inhabitants must have been grateful indeed. The animals being secured in the pounds, occasion was taken to inspect, count and mark them. 'Trespassers' were held for a year and a day, and if not claimed were forfeit to the King, or to the lord to whom he had leased the forest. It is recorded, for instance, that in 1355 the Earl of Marsh claimed for strays in the forests of Clarendon, Melchet, Groveley and Buckholt.

In Coke's time, there were sixty-nine royal forests, in which the hunting was reserved to the King. From then on, disafforestation was rapid, and by 1850 only four, as to-day, remained, the forests of Windsor, Wolmer, New Forest, and the Forest of Dean. Only the last two retain their Courts of Verderers and their pounds, and only in the New Forest are drifts still made. Today, of course, the royal prerogative is very much diminished, and the sovereign no longer hunts deer in the Royal Forests.

New Forest

This account is derived from information provided by the New Forest Pony Breeding and Cattle Society.

There are fifteen or more New Forest pounds, all built in post-and-rail on a similar plan: rectangular, with usually a gate at either end, and containing a small compartment known as a 'crush', used to control animals for necessary proceedings.

Pony and cattle drifts are held in each of the three districts, usually in autumn. All the animals are rounded up and driven to the pounds, to be inspected and receive any necessary attention. There they are marked, and their tails are cut to a distinctive shape according to the district where they belong. Cattle are also earmarked with a different coloured tag each year.

Until the perimeter of the Forest was fenced about 1964 there were pounds at Lymington, Totton, Sandford (outside Ringwood) and Fordingbridge, where Forest animals that wandered, known as lane creepers, were regularly impounded, and their owners fined for allowing them to stray. These pounds were brick-built, with one gate and usually a hayrack. Animals found unlawfully depastured on the Forest are still impounded, but usually in the Agister's (Forest official) field, not in the Forest pounds, which are not secure and have no provision for feeding and watering.

The historic Court of Swainmote, (the court for the people of the Forest) is held yearly to deal with offences under the bye-laws.

Two examples of Forest pounds are described under Hampshire in the Gazetteer.

Forest of Dean

Much of the information which follows is taken from the work of C. E. Hart.[48]

The inhabitants of the forest have had rights therein from time immemorial. It is recorded that in 1688 pounds for cattle were ordered to be built at some convenient place in the Lea Bailey at a cost not exceeding £3. There was trouble, of course; in 1696, for example, ten persons were outlawed for poundbreach and riot in Dean Forest: the said persons being very poor and having submitted themselves. So it continued, until in 1898 Samuel Virgo was convicted at Coleford for poundbreach at the Speech House.

There was constant friction between the Crown and the commoners, the former mainly concerned with planting (Dean Forest was traditionally an important source of timber for the Navy), the latter with their rights; and the miners of Dean were a tough crew. A frequent cause of trouble was the sheep which the commoners insisted it was their traditional right to graze in the forest, and similar rights were demanded for swine. As late as 1929, a man was convicted under the Pound Breach Act of 1843 for releasing twenty sheep impounded by a Crown official. (The conviction was quashed because it was not proved that the enclosure in which they were found was enclosed land within the meaning of the Act).

Between 1860 and 1866 the fines collected for animals impounded because found illegally in enclosures devoted to forestry fell from £34. 14. 7 to £3. 3. 0 with no reason given. It may have been because the practice regarding stock in the forest was changing; evidently there were fewer 'trespassers'. The last recorded drift was during the Winter Heyning of 1862, when the fines were still those of 1778, plus one shilling for donkeys and mules. A 70-year old commoner said in 1904: 'The Crown used to drive to Pound all that could be found in the Forest about July once a year. I have had to pay a shilling each for ponies at the Pound, Whites Lodge, Kensley'. It is believed that the custom ceased because of the expense of holding the drift, which certainly suggests that animals were fewer.

Until the 1950's four official pounds continued in use, each with its pound keeper: Connop, Park Pike, Herbert Lodge, and Brandrick's Green at Moseley Green. Animals found in the enclosures were impounded by the Crown officials. The owner had to pay 4d 'for turning the key of the lock'; for sheep 6d or 1s, increased in 1949 to 2s and 5s; for cattle and horses 5s, pigs 5s, increased if the offence was repeated. The pound keeper had the 'lock fees', the Crown the remainder, the commoners protesting that they could only legally be charged the lock fee.

From about 1950 still fewer animals were being kept in the forest, there was less reason to apprehend strays, and the pounds gradually fell out of use. At present (1976) only the Park Pike pound (an excellent specimen) (Fig. 11)

16

is kept in repair and occasionally used; at Brandrick's Green scanty remains can with difficulty be found, and the others have totally disappeared, so rapidly are traces of old custom obliterated.

Dartmoor Forest

Dartmoor, bleak, largely bare of trees, illustrates perfectly that land technically 'forest' was not necessarily woodland, wholly or in part. Strictly, the Forest of Dartmoor comprises the 70,000 acres owned by the Duchy of Cornwall, the rest of Dartmoor being distinguished as the Commons of Devon, owned by the lords of the manors, and the whole is subject to common rights, which have obtained for many centuries.

Among the many ancient features of Dartmoor is the historic Dunnabridge Pound, long central to the practices of the moor. In 1342, the Bailiff or Reeve of the manor of Dartmoor 'takes credit for the repair of the pound at Dunnabridge'[49]. In a tithe dispute in 1627 a witness said:

> There are about 35 ancient tenements within the Forest ... and the tenants have been accustomed, time out of mind, to make three several drifts yearly for cattle and one for horses depasturing upon the said Forest of Dartmoor to Dynabridge pound, and are there to attend two or three days and nights for the watering and depasturing of the said cattle near the said pound and to drive such as are not owned to Lydford as estrays, and every of the said tenants is to have upon bringing of the said cattle and horses to Dynabridge pound a halfpenny loaf and that such as make default of such service to forfeit 6s 8d.[50]

In 1631 Sir Thomas Reynell gave a somewhat different account:

> It has been customary to make four drifts for cattle in the Forest of Dartmoor, in the four several parts of the Forest, at any time after 23rd of June and before 6th August. The cattle are driven to a pound called Donnabridge Pound if they are found in the east, west or south quarters of the Forest, and if found in the north quarter to a pound called Creber Pound ... There was a drift made in the north quarter on Monday 15th July, and amongst other things a black ox was driven to Creber pound. It was not challenged or claimed and was accordingly driven to the Castle of Lydford, and proclaimed and not claimed and adjudged to the King as an estray ... and according to the usage of the said Forest was appraised by three or four tenants of the Forest at a value of 56s 8d.[51]

Dunnabridge Pound is about two and a half miles east of Two Bridges on the Ashburton Road. It is nearly circular, and encloses an area of about two acres with a drystone rubble wall rising to about 5½ feet. The last Pound-keeper was named Dinah Tuckett, and was the last occupant of Dunnabridge Pound Farm. The little field beside it was known as Play Park, said to be where the men wrestled to while away the time during the drifts. Drifts continued to be made until the 1930's, since when Dunnabridge Pound has fallen out of use. There is another pound, however, on the moor, which may still be used, and is kept in readiness, though the poundkeeper now usually finds it convenient to graze strays on his own farm instead of hand-feeding them in the pound. This is the manor pound of Spitchwick, at Pound-gate. The manor court is still active, and was excluded from recent legislation designed to abolish obsolete courts.[52]

Exmoor Forest

For this account I am indebted to the work of E. T. MacDermot.[53]

The ancient Forest pound was at Withypool. Nine drifts were held each year: horses five, cattle three, sheep one. Stock was pounded for counting, marking, inspection, and the identification of 'trespassers'. Unclaimed or un-redeemed sheep were forfeited to the forester after nine days; cattle and ponies were kept in a field adjoining the pound for a year and a day. In 1678, William Williams, aged 49, Poundkeeper, deposed that eight years previously an Irish bullock was forfeited for not being claimed in time. [The site of Withypool Pound is still recognisable. G.R. 846354].

The leasee of the Forest built and enclosed a new farm at Simonsbath about the middle of the seventeenth century, about sixteen miles from Withy-pool, and it soon became the principal forest pound, though Withypool pound was used for another century at least. The new pound was built between the farm and the old course of the road from Exford to the bridge, only separated by the road from the Barle. [The small piece of partially fenced land at G.R. 772392 fits this account]. Simonsbath pound was mended as late as 1817, at which time the poundherd was paid £2 per annum.

Exmoor was let out on lease by the King from 1508 onwards. The rent of £46 13s 4d was unaltered until the last lease expired in 1814. This was the end of the Forest in the old sense, for in 1818 the property was sold to one Knight for £50,000 and divided into 296 portions.

In addition to the official Forest pounds, there were doubtless village pounds for local use. One such survives at Brompton Regis.

Epping Forest

Epping Forest, with Hainault Forest, were from their beginning parts of the Forest of Waltham, and are all that remains of it.

The story of the fight against illegal enclosure of Epping Forest by the lords of the manors, and especially the part played by the Willingale family, is famous. The struggle ended in disafforestation, and the Epping Forest Act of 1878, which acquired all the rights of the lords of the manors, and appointed

The Corporation of the City of London as Conservator, all rights of common being continued.

The Superintendent of Epping Forest has kindly provided information about present day practice. Animals are marked with the mark of one of the twelve parishes before being turned out. Six pounds are maintained; two Conservators' and four Commoners'. (For details see gazetteer under Essex). Nowadays it is rare for impounded animals not to be claimed. When this does occur, a notice is published in one or more of the local papers, stating that unless claimed within seven days of publication the animal or animals will be sold by public auction, and the proceeds of the sale after payment of expenses handed over to the Conservators.

Hainault Forest

Hainault Forest was disafforested and enclosed in 1851, and the splendid timber ruthlessly exploited. Part of it was later bought back from the Crown, and now, with Epping Forest, is a valued playground for Londoners. One excellent pound is preserved, and bears a notice: POUND Circa 1904. Erected for impounding stray cattle in Hainault Forest. It does not seem to have been used in recent years, and is probably maintained for its historic interest.

No information has come to light about pounds or impounding in other forests, such as the Forests of Wyre and Savernake.

THE FATE OF THE POUND

As the need diminished, the practice of distraint being otherwise catered for, and straying animals usually accommodated in a yard or field, most parishes have lost their pound. Many, especially wooden ones, just decayed or fell down, and many are still becoming finally derelict. Many others were deliberately destroyed. Few people know that it is still illegal to damage a pound, and the offence may cost them £20. Perhaps the biggest enemy of pounds at the present time is the Highway Authority, and many have been cleared away in the cause of road widening. A recent sad case was that of Newton Flotman (Norfolk), which it was understood was to be preserved, but which unexpectedly disappeared in favour of a hideous concrete bank. A number of pounds now enjoy 'listed' status, and it is to be hoped that the present enthusiasm for conservation will save most of the surviving examples.

19

As long ago as 1888 a contributor to Notes and Queries spoke a severe warning:[54]

'Day by day (Oh, for the shades of Mr Pickwick!) the common pounds of the kingdom, once so well known in every lordship, township and village, are, through the greed of landowners and the unwakefulness of the tenants of the manor, being lessened down and swept away. Having marked that not so long ago a seeker was by your readers afforded a knowledge of the places at which stocks were still kept to frown a warning on wrongdoers, I deemed that perhaps the like help might be given me in telling the tale of pounds. Meanwhile it would be as well for such as look upon these with an evil eye to bear in mind there is little or no question that the overthrow of the pound is a nuisance at common law, indictable as against the peace of the Queen'.

It is sometimes possible to determine, within a little, when a pound fell out of use. Dates range from about 1850: Canon Pyon (Herefordshire) to Compton Martin (Somerset) about 1924. Mr Bernard Lodge, of Dartford (Kent), who was born in 1890, gives an eyewitness account of impounding:

I used to pass it each day on my way to the National School a little further up the hill . . . the old pound in which all kinds of animals – horses, cattle, sheep, pigs and donkeys found straying on the highway were impounded until claimed by their owners.

It was fun to see the efforts of the police and passers-by trying to get them in, but less fun for the owner, after being fined, getting them out.[55]

Eighty seven year old Mrs Loft's account in the same year (1969) probably refers to a makeshift after the demolition of the wooden pound described by Mr Lodge: 'There used to be a rough bit of ground on the corner called the pound. My father had the key of this place and many a time I have heard him knocked up for someone to put a stray animal in there'.

Here and there, local enthusiasm has secured the restoration and preservation of the village pound. Among examples where recent good rescue work may be seen are: Ryton (Co. Durham) (Fig. 7), Field Broughton (Lancashire), Gimingham and North Elmham (Norfolk) (Fig. 8), Batheaston (Fig. 19) and Fivehead (Somerset), Hambledon (Surrey), Sidlesham and Wilmington (Sussex), Berkswell and Eastcote (Warwickshire), Bromyard (Herefordshire), Follifoot and Spaunton (Yorkshire). Elsewhere, the pound has been saved, whole or in part, by incorporation in an adjacent garden, or roofed and converted to a garage, store, or even a public convenience! At Pershore (Worcestershire) there is an example, probably unique, of complete rebuilding of a derelict pound, following the dimensions and description recorded by a local enthusiast. It is a pleasure to record that in a number of places – but not enough – plans for restoration are afoot. Slowly, very slowly, it is being realised that we cannot afford to lose any more of our heritage, to neglect or to the developer, it matters not which.

20

LOCKUPS

One reason for including lockups in this study is that in a number of places, among them Clophill (Bedfordshire), Swaffham Prior (Cambridgeshire), Orsett (Essex) (Fig. 12), Breedon on the Hill (Leicestershire), Docking (Norfolk), Hunmanby (Yorkshire) (Fig. 13), the pound, to confine animals, and the lockup, to serve the same function for humans, form one complex.

In comparison with the antiquity of the village pound, the lockup is almost a newcomer. The earliest reference to it I have detected is dated 1563 (below). Intended for the temporary custody of such as were 'caught in the act', or suspects, or drunks and rowdies, perhaps, it is variously known as lockup, blind house, round house, cage, or clink, (a multiplicity of terms inconvenient to a scanner of indices!) It is parish property, provided at the discretion of the Vestry or the Corporation, and is not a gaol, or one of the Houses of Correction introduced under the Poor Law Act of 1576. The distinction is that the occupant of the lockup is still to be brought to trial. Responsibility for his custody rests on the constable, that is, the holder, often unwilling, of the ancient unpaid parish office. Barking (London) was exceptionally well provided by the end of the sixteenth century with both a cage and a House of Correction.

A typical lockup is round, windowless except perhaps for one or more small slits towards the summit, the roof domed to prevent rescue, a stout wooden door reinforced with iron or studded with nails, often with a grille inserted in or above it: a bleak and cheerless place indeed in which to spend even one night. Other lockups are square or rectangular, and some contain two cells: Swaffham Prior (Cambridgeshire), Paignton (Devon), Bishop's Castle (Shropshire), Bathford (Somerset), Bradford on Avon (Fig. 18) and Trowbridge (Wiltshire), and Hunmanby (Yorkshire) (Fig. 13). One example, at Hartlip Hill (Kent) was adapted as a two-roomed dwelling for an old woman, until it disappeared in the cause of road widening.

A few lockups, including Bradford on Avon, where there is also a chimney, have iron bedsteads fixed to the wall. A bench affords a lesser degree of comfort. There is a curious arrangement, perhaps unique, at Bradwell on Sea (Essex) (Fig. 17), where the doorposts are adapted with a shaped and hinged iron bar to secure the wrists of captives, pillorywise, to the number of five, including a very small clasp at the bottom, suggesting provision for a very small prisoner!

In some towns a room in the Town Hall was utilised: Alcester (Warwickshire), Wincanton and Somerton (Somerset), Chippenham (Wiltshire). Perhaps in accordance with civic dignity, town lockups tend to be more impressive than the simple 'cage', though a mere cell in the basement might do.

At Moreton in Marsh (Gloucestershire) and Fenstanton (Huntingdonshire) the lockup is in the clock tower. Among oddities are the lockups of Winsford (Cheshire) in the base of the village cross, Geddington (Northamptonshire) similarly placed in the Eleanor Cross; and Iron Acton (Gloucestershire) where there is a small cell in the base of the church tower, entered from within the church. At Pembridge (Herefordshire) the lockup is in the roof of the market cross, access by ladder.

Recollections of the lockup at Wincanton (Somerset) about 1850 are to be read in Sweetman's history of the town:[56]

> On the west side of the Town Hall, before the enlargement of 1867, down a step or two, was a miserable room about seven or eight feet square, and incongruously called 'Roundhouse', or more fittingly 'blind house', as its only light was through a grill in the door about six or seven inches square. There was no attempt made to keep it wholesome, and the only bedding was a heap of straw. Into this hole two or more prisoners were put and kept day after day, with rats for company. More than one poor wretch has died there. I remember two such cases.

Perhaps it is legitimate to hope that such conditions were exceptionally horrible, if only because the parish would be held responsible for death in custody. That they were not unique is shewn by an account of the lockup in Swindon:

> The 'Blind house' was at the top of Newport Street. A dark and dingy hole, about eight feet square with no light or ventilation, except a grating eight inches square in the doorway. There was a stone floor to this place, and a wooden bench fastened into the wall. There was no other accommodation or convenience whatever. A navvy building the Great Western Railway was got out by digging a channel under the door. [57]

Among references to the lockup are the following from the borough records of Calne.[58]

1581 Lock, staples and hasp for the cage doors 2s 4d; to old Wickwar for covering the cage 4d. To Jonas Alexander for tiling the cage viis.

1655 For hooks and a staple for the cage 1s 4d. Boards and nails about the stocks and blindhouse.

1656 To Richard Willis for a sack of lime for the blind house 1s 8d; for tiles for the blind house 1s 10d; to John Garraway and his son for 2 days labour on the house 4s; to John Dash for lasts and nails used about the house 2s; for hair lime for the same 6d.

1676 12 horseloads of stone to the Marsh and 12 horseloads of mortar to mend the cage 2s 6d; for board to mend the blindhouse and cage 9s.

'Board' seems costly compared to stone and mortar. The existence of a blind-house and a cage at the same time is a puzzle. Unfortunately, Calne has lost both.

There are several entries in the borough records of Chippenham[59] relating to the lockup, among them:

1563 Item for a key to the blynd house dore vid

1629 Item, paid for making cleane the blindhouse viid.

1709 Spent with the six piratts in custody . . . 1s 0d for 7 quarts of ale.

Presumably, one man, one quart. It is sad to reflect that curiosity about this interesting episode will never be satisfied.

It is clear from parish and borough records and other documentary sources that the lockup was once a familiar sight, though probably not ubiquitous, as the pound was. It went out of use after about the middle of the nineteenth century, as an organised police force developed, and police stations were built. Relatively few remain, compared to the number of pounds still existing, but such as survive are nearly always kept in repair, a matter of local pride. There is here a contrast with the recent sad fate of so many pounds. Wiltshire, with thirteen examples, is exceptionally well supplied, and Somerset is not far behind.

It is good that these relics should be preserved, not only for their interest as structures, but as a lasting reminder of the harshness of our not-so-distant past.

Fig. 9 : Southampton

23

As it would be absurd to attribute pounds to 'Avon' or 'Humberside', entries are listed under the historic counties, before the mutilations and obliterations of 1974.

The terms pound and pinfold, which are interchangeable, are here applied as commonly used in the individual counties. There is, of course, some overlap.

For location, rather than a pedantic adherence to one system only, I have adopted what seems the quickest and most convenient method for each case, often by reference to direction and distance (as the crow flies) from familiar towns, to numbered roads and conspicuous crossroads, and sometimes by four-figure Grid References. For really obscure remains a six-figure reference is indispensable.

The letter C denotes examples not recorded personally, but derived from correspondents. The letters N.P. indicate descriptions found in Sir Nikolaus Pevsner's The Buildings of England. All others I have visited.

The record was made between 1973 and 1978.

Fig. 10 : Anstey, Leics.

BEDFORDSHIRE

POUNDS

CLOPHILL. Crossroads A6/A418. Opposite village green, behind the Flying Horse.
Rectangular. Brick, with good oak gate. Lockup adjacent.

WOBURN. 6 miles N.E. of Leighton Buzzard. Corner of Leighton Road and Timber Lane.
Rectangular. Post and rails. Decaying (1975).

Remains: Blunham, Upper Gravenhurst (stored).

LOCKUPS

CLOPHILL. Adjoins pound.
Brick, slate roof. Wooden door with iron grille above.

HARROLD. 8 miles N.W. of Bedford. GR9456. On green.
Excellent round cage, stone built with finely corbelled roof. Stout wooden door.
Small light.

SILSO. (N.P). 8 miles S of Bedford.
Octagonal, with pointed arch to doorway.

TURVEY. A. 428, 7 miles W of Bedford. May Road.
Stone, slate roof. Slit window in E gable. Much altered, with modern doors.

BERKSHIRE

POUNDS

BUCKLEBURY. 5 miles N.E. of Newbury. Chapel Row Hill, opposite Brown's Gate.
Rectangular. Good brick walls, but S.E. corner falling (1974).

SPEEN. 1½ miles N.W. of Newbury. Corner of A4 and Pound (Church) Lane.
Rectangular. Wooden post and rails. Needs repair (1976).

WALTHAM S. LAWRENCE. (C). 8 miles E.N.E. of Reading. By Church entrance.
Very fine post and rails, with truncated corners.

Remains or site: Lower and Upper Basildon, Blewbury, Hungerford, Marcham, Thatcham.

LOCKUP

PANGBOURNE. In garden of Church Cottage (which was the home of Kenneth Grahame).
Circular. Brick, tiled roof, with wide eaves and weathervane, tiny light in dome. Door
up steps original, timber-framed, studded, timbers horizontal, two original bolts.
Grille.

BUCKINGHAMSHIRE

POUNDS

FINGEST. 7 miles N.W. of Gt. Marlow. Lane N. of Church, by drive gates.
Square. Iron bars, square section, on brick base. Top bar 5' above base. Lower half has
two additional 1" bars, so small animals are very secure! A notable example.

HARDWICK. A413, 5 miles N of Aylesbury. Opposite green.
Area about quarter acre, bounded by wooden fence, brick wall and hurdles.

WEST WYCOMBE. A40 at W end of village.
Irregular quadrilateral bounded by wooden post and rails and brick wall. At one point
lower rail is absent, allowing passage of small animals into field. Contains transformer.

Site: Askett. N end of Pillar Box Lane.
Small square wooden post and rail structure, without entrance. Plaque: site of Askett
pound.

Buckinghamshire—cont.

AMERSHAM. Within the Market Hall of 1682. The arches of the N.E. corner (elsewhere open) are bricked up, E facing one fitted with a semi-circular grille. Cell rectangular. Door in S wall opens into the covered space: original, studded, with semi-circular grille.

GREAT MISSENDEN. A413, 6 miles N.W. of Amersham. S of town, E side of street. Rectangular, with rear corners truncated. Brick, 3 overhanging courses at eaves, small grille. Tiled pyramidal roof, with tiled copings at angles. 4' entrance, probably modern.

WEST WYCOMBE. At bottom of Church Lane, and part of a very ancient timbered complex. Horizontal timbers, very old studded door. Barred window above.

Remains: Beaconsfield—Market Place, grille in W corner of N wall of Hall Barn Estate Office.

CAMBRIDGESHIRE

POUNDS

BOTTISHAM. 6 miles E.N.E. of Cambridge. Lode Road, adjoining Pound Cottage. Rectangular. Rubble, corners buttressed. Roofed and used as garage.

COTTENHAM. B1049, 6 miles N of Cambridge. W side of High Street. Large rectangle. Brick, side fronting street lowered. Restored.

COVENEY. 3 miles N.W. of Ely. In very small village, miles from anywhere. Square. Brick. Well restored.

LANDBEACH. 5 miles N.E. of Cambridge. By Church. Irregular quadrilateral. Brick.

SWAFFHAM PRIOR. B1102, 8 miles N.E. of Cambridge. On Cage Hill. Rectangular. Rubble and brick. Built 1830. Contains lockup and fire engine house.

WEST WRATTING. B1052, 7 miles S.W. of Newmarket. In High Street. Square. Low brick walls. Notice reads: Church Property.

WILBURTON. A1123, 5 miles S.W. of Ely. N of road, E end of village. Large rectangle. Brick. Needs some repair (1973). Used in living memory.

Remains: Stretham.

LOCKUPS

BURWELL. B1102, 10 miles N.E. of Cambridge. N end of village. Brick, tiled roof, slit window high on E. wall, modern double doors. 'Early nineteenth century. Originally two cells with separate doors; over each a shallow grille' (Royal Commission on Historical Monuments).

COVENEY? Small brick building abutting on pound, but not intrinsic.

SWAFFHAM PRIOR. In the pound. Two cells, studded doors, oval barred window over.

CHESHIRE

PINFOLDS

ASHTON BY BUDWORTH. (C). S.W. corner of field at junction of Cann Lane and Knuts-ford Road. Square, with 4½' stone walls. Three in good condition, the fourth, which contained the entrance, partly destroyed (1966).

Cheshire—cont.

BICKERTON. (C). A534 near top of Gallentry Bank.
Rectangular, with 5½' walls. Sandstone. No gate.

CAPENHURST GREEN. Capenhurst Lane opposite the green.
Rectangular. Coursed sandstone blocks, with stone coping. Stone gateposts. No gate.

HOOLE VILLAGE. (C). N.E. side of Oak Lane next Smithy Cottage.
Rectangular. Sandstone. No gate; opening is to curtilage of Smithy Cottage.

SPITAL (LOWER BEBINGTON). (C). W. side of Brimstage Road just over 100 yards W of Spital Crossroads.
Rectangular. Stone, roughly coursed, massive stone gateposts and coping, with gate. Floor concreted. Contains water trough. Plaque: This is the old/spital pinfold/or pound/used for the/impounding/of stray cattle.

Remains or site: Poole, Wardle.

A descriptive list was kindly provided by the Cheshire County Council.

LOCKUPS

KELSALL. (N.P). 10 miles N.E. of Chester. Opposite Royal Oak.
Big stone blocks. Windowless.

WINSFORD. (C). A54, 5 miles S of Northwich. Delamere Street, Over.
In the large (9') stepped stone base of the village cross, entered through a small door in one side.

CORNWALL

POUNDS

CHACEWATER. A390, 5 miles W of Truro, W of village, S side of road, just W of sideroad from S. Day. GR 744442.
Square, walls to 8'. Drystone, large blocks, with massive effect. No coping. Good entrance towards road (10 yards back, uphill). Overgrown. One side beginning to fall. (1977).

GWITHIAN. 4 miles N.E. of Hayle, N of Church, corner of green.
Circular banked enclosure said to be just one-third acre. Very overgrown with brambles, and difficult to identify. A pity. Believed to be the hundred pound.

LESNEWTH. 3 miles E of Boscastle. E of Church, in grounds of Old Rectory.
Circular, internal diameter 30'. 8' wall, inserted into hillside, banked opposite. Slabby local stone laid flat, with internal overhang at summit. Stone right gatepost. Left side of entrance decaying. Condition otherwise excellent. An interesting example, possibly a hundred pound.

TUCOYS. 1 mile W of Constantine, in lane ½ mile W of B3291. GR 712292.
Irregular quadrilateral, side to road 30'. Drystone, narrow entrance, stone gateposts. Somewhat overgrown (1977).

Remains or site: Antony, Carn Ennis, Coombe, Rame, S. Michael Caerhayes, Tregony.

LOCKUPS (CLINKS)

CALLINGTON. Rectangular? Front 8' x 10' high. Good flat-arched entrance. Not accessible.

GRAMPOUND. Small lean-to behind Town Hall. No light or grille. Door not original.

Remains or site: Fowey. Two grilles in wall of old building now part of Town Hall.

CUMBERLAND

PINFOLDS

KIRKANDREWES ON EDEN. (C). At junction of roads to Carlisle, Bowness, Burgh on Sands.
Rhomboidal, longest side 34 yards, opposite side two houses. Random stone. One wall 5', completed by section of new wall, the other sides lowered. The houses and their gardens look to be encroachments. Contains electrical sub-station.

S. BEES. (C). Pinfold Yard, Oldrigg S. Bees.
Rectangular. High stone wall. Cared for. Previously used by Local Authority; now as car standing in exchange for minimal rent and upkeep.

DERBYSHIRE

PINFOLDS

BARLOW. 3½ miles N.W. of Chesterfield. GR 343746.
Square. Front wall coursed, walls 6'. Remarkable for window opening on low sill, closed with three horizontal wooden bars.

BARROW ON TRENT. B5009, S of Derby. Church Lane.
Rectangular, backing on to brick building. Good coursed masonry.

BIGGIN. GR 155593.
Circular, drystone wall with coping. Entrance broken down, otherwise good (1975).

BONSALL. 2 miles S.W. of Matlock. E side of Yeoman Street, garden of Pinfold Cottage.
Large rectangle, rough drystone walls to 10'. Backs on to rock cliff.

BRADFIELD. 4 miles N.W. of Sheffield. GR 269923.
Large rectangle, coursed stone with coping. Original entrance to lane closed, new entrance to field closed with hurdle. In use for some purpose.

CALOW. 2 miles E of Chesterfield. Opposite side of road before reaching Somerset House Hotel from Chesterfield.
Part of garden of cottage. Square. Rubble, partly coursed. New entrance. Wall opening has held 4 wooden bars, as at Barlow.

CURBAR. E of A619, 8 miles W of Chesterfield. GR 250746. Opposite bottom of Pinfold Hill.
Circular, 8' walls, roughly coursed, with coping. Modern gate. Used by local Council for storage.

EGGINTON. 6 miles S.W. of Derby, off B5009. Corner of Duck Street.
Rectangular. Massive stone walls of roughly dressed blocks. Opposite entrances with ornamental iron gates. Quite a seemly conversion.

HATHERSAGE. A625, 6 miles S.W. of Sheffield. Beside Church Bank.
High front wall rebuilt. On door: The old village pinfold. Back wall collapsed. Neglected (1975).

HOPE. A625, 2 miles E of Castleton. GR 172833.
Circular, rough drystone walls. Repaired 1976. A rare example of a pinfold still in use.

MACKWORTH. A52, 2 miles N.W. of Derby. Rocky Lane, W of Church, standing back from lane.
Rectangular. Massive drystone wall, with semi-circular coping. Used as garden.

MILLTOWN. N of B6014, 3 miles N.W. of Matlock. Opposite Miners' Arms.
Square. Drystone walls deteriorating. Stone jambs to entrance. Restoration intended (1975).

OVER HADDON. 1½ miles S.W. of Bakewell. GR 203665. W end of village by green.
Square. Drystone walls, stone jambs to entrance.

TIDESWELL. B6049, 5 miles N.E. of Buxton. S end of village, by Pinfold Close Estate.
Irregular quadrilateral. Drystone walls, wooden door. Used as garden.

Derbyshire—cont.

YOULGREAVE. A524, 3 miles S of Bakewell. Immediately W of the Methodist Chapel which is in use (another is not).
Large rectangle. Drystone with semi-circular coping. Restored and some building taking place within. No access (1975).

Remains: Brassington, Butterton, Chellaston, Chelmorton, Elton, Grindleford, Grindon, Harthill, Hartington, Hassop, Ible, Monyash, Thorpe, Wardlow.

LOCKUPS

ALFRETON. (C). 8 miles S.W. of Mansfield. King Street.
Rectangular. Stone, pitched roof with stone slabs, circular openings. 'House of Confinement' carved over door. Believed to date from about 1820.

CURBAR. (See entry under pinfolds). (N.P). S side of street, at top end of village.
Circular, with conical roof.

SMISBY. (N.P). 2 miles N of Ashby de la Zouch. Close to Tournament Field.
Octagonal. Brick, studded door, roof a spire with ball.

TICKNALL. (N.P). A514, 5 miles N of Ashby de la Zouch, near Church.
Circular, with pointed polygonal roof and studded door.

DEVON

POUNDS

BICTON. A376, 4 miles N.E. of Budleigh Salterton, at corner of approach road to S. Mary's Church.
Rectangular. Rubble, cement-capped. 8' walls. Modern iron gate.

DUNNABRIDGE. (C). A384, 4 miles E of Two Bridges.
Roughly circular, enclosing about 2 acres. Drystone rubble wall, about 5½' in height. On inside face, slight suggestion of earthen bank beneath. Entrance gated, of paled construction. Contains stone seat roofed with granite slab. The ancient Dartmoor pound.

NORTH BOVEY. N entrance to village.
Large rectangle, with 8' walls. Massive random walling. Roofed with corrugated iron.

NORTHAM. N of Bideford. Between 56 and 60 Cross Street.
Rectangular, walls 8'. Slabby local stone, long side to street rendered. 7' entrance closed by tall wooden gate. Roofed extension to W, with remarkable circular pillar at centre of entrance to extension.

POUNDSGATE. N side of A384, 4 miles N.W. of Ashburton.
Rectangular. Drystone, large, roughly dressed blocks. The manor pound of Spitchwick (Widecombe in the Moor).

S. GILES IN THE WOOD. 3 miles E of Torrington, at High Bullen. 200 yards E of crossing. GR 535202.
Long narrow rectangle. Local stone, with some coursing. Brick corners, and brick pilasters at entrance. Gable of concrete blocks added to support tin roof.

TORRINGTON (GREAT). Castle Hill, opposite bowling green.
Rectangular. Random stone, very substantial walls to 8'. Modern wooden gate. Contains large hut used as changing room.

SIDBURY. At Pound Close, E side of Sidmouth Road.
Square. Random stone, with brick corners. W side rebuilt.

WOODBURY. 8 miles S.E. of Exeter, 1 mile E of Woodbury, at crossing of B3180.
Quadrangular. Brick, capped with semi-circular sandstone. Corner recently (April 1977) demolished by lorry.

Remains or site: East Budleigh, Peter Tavy.

Devon—cont.

NORTH TAWTON. (C). 7 miles N.E. of Okehampton. N of A3072. In Essington, below the Council Office, formerly the Justices' Court.
Stone built, leaded light windows, iron grille in door.

PAIGNTON. (C). Junction of Littlegate Road and Mill Lane, adjacent to Princes Street.
Thick stone walls, vaulted roof, 8' high in centre. Two cells, each 7' by 6'. Tiny slit window. Restored 1976. The last prisoner, about 1860, locked up for stealing cider, said to have hanged himself.

DORSET

POUNDS

ASHMORE. B3081, 5 miles S.E. of Shaftesbury, 100 yards S.W. of Church.
Irregular. Stone, but separated from farmyard by wall of concrete blocks which has evidently reduced the area.

CORFE CASTLE. A351, 6 miles S.E. of Wareham. E side of Swanage Road adjacent to barn with outside staircase.
Square. Rubble, roughly coursed. Wooden door. Needs repair (1974).

HOLNEST. E side of A352, 4 miles S.E. of Sherborne, quarter mile N of church.
Square. Rubble with vertical coping. Ivy-covered and decaying (1974). Used as shed.

LANGTON MATRAVERS. 8 miles S.E. of Wareham, W end of village, behind Manor Pound Cottage.
Square. Portland stone, walls 6', carefully maintained. Old entrance from lane built up, and new one made into garden of the haywarden's cottage, of which it now forms part. In use until between the wars. A good example of conservation.

PORTLAND. 200 yards S.E. of S. George's Church.
Rectangular. Random stone walls 5–6', with irregular vertical coping. Stone lintel. Used within living memory, fines collected by constable. The court still meets. Pound moved a short distance 'after the war'.

STALBRIDGE. A357, 7 miles E of Sherborne, S of main crossroads near Stalbridge Arms.
Irregular quadrilateral. Coursed rubble with cement capping. Walls lowered. Contains public telephone.

WAREHAM. Corner of Pound Lane, on line of town wall.
Rectangular. Brick, with iron gate. Notice by the Steward of the Manor of Wareham, the Court Leet of which still meets. Very well maintained.

WOOL. A352, 5 miles W of Wareham. Bindon Lane, N side of junction with Station Road.
Square. Brick, with brick pillars to entrance.

Remains or site: Bishop's Caundle, Buckland Newton, E. Orchard, E. Stoke, Frome Vauchurch, Langton Matravers (2), Poole (elaborate inscribed pillar at junction of Pound Lane and Fernside Road), Shaftesbury.

LOCKUPS

GILLINGHAM. 70 yards S of Church. N. side of South Street.
Rectangular. Coursed rubble with tiled roof. 4-centred head to doorway. Interior lined with brick. Modern entrance in gable end.

POOLE. S.E. side of Sarum Street, Thames Mews, adjoins Town Cellars.
Rectangular, 25' by 8'. Coursed stone. Large blocks surround doors and small windows. Slate roof. Dated 1820. Wide door on short side inserted on conversion to engine house.

SWANAGE. (C). N of Town Hall.
Rectangular. Ashlar with stone tiled roof. Ancient door, nail-studded. Barrel vaulted. Small window with grille. Above door: Erected for the Prevention of Vice and Immorality by the Friends of Religion and Good Order A.D. 1803.

Dorset—cont.

Remains: Lyme Regis. Door of lockup. Okeford Fitzpaine. 2 miles S of Sturminster Newton. The Cross. The door of the lockup, iron-studded, with small grille in arched head, set in timber frame, is in wall of modern thatched cottage, on original site.

COUNTY DURHAM

PINFOLDS

RYTON ON TYNE. (C). 6 miles W of Newcastle. W of village green, beginning of Westfield Lane.
Irregular. Roughly coursed stone with coping. Contains manger, and small stream beneath cobbled floor. Restored 1974. An exceptionally good example.

CRAWCROOK. (C). 1 mile W of Ryton. S side of Paygate Crossroads.
Lost some area in the 1950's for road-widening. Used as Council depot.

Remains: Cleadon.

ESSEX

POUNDS

EPPING FOREST. Information from the Superintendent of Epping Forest.

Conservators' Pounds

Oak Hill, Woodford. Large rectangle, about 30 x 50 yards. Iron uprights, corner posts and bars. Wooden gates.
Nursery Road, Loughton. Rectangle 33 x 47 yards. Iron uprights and bars, corner posts oak. Wooden gates.

Parish Pounds

Warren Drive, Loughton. Rectangular. Divided longitudinally into two.
Jubilee Retreat, Bury Road, Chingford. Also divided into two.
Brook Road, Buckhurst Hill. Rectangular.
Blakehall Road, Wanstead. Rectangular.

All the parish pounds are constructed in oak.

LAMBOURNE END (HAINAULT FOREST). (C). Heavy iron post and rails, bearing a wooden sign: POUND/Circa 1904/Erected for impounding stray/cattle in Hainault Forest.

ORSETT. (C). 3 miles N of Tilbury. Re-sited on green with lockup.
Fine wooden post-and-rails (4) complete. The lower half has added verticals to restrain small animals.

SAFFRON WALDEN. Little Walden Road at top of common.
Squarish. Brick, with semi-circular coping, except E wall, which is flint. Brick arch over spiked wooden door. Bought by Borough Council from the Lord of the Manor (Lord Braybrooke) in 1958 for £5. Needs some repair (1975).

Remains: Shalford.

LOCKUPS

BRADWELL ON SEA. (C). S.E. corner of churchyard.
Square, brick, pyramidal tiled roof. Wooden door with grille. Wooden doorposts comprise one half of pillory (to grasp wrist) the other being a shaped and padlocked iron bar. Built 1817 to replace earlier cage. Restored 1966.

CANEWDON. (N.P). S of River Crouch. By E entrance to churchyard. Small weatherboarded shed, 1775. Stocks within.

Essex—cont.

ORSETT. (C). 4 miles N of Tilbury. Rebuilt on green.
Wooden, weatherboarded, pyramidal roof. Small barred window.

TOLLESBURY. (N.P). 7 miles E.N.E. of Maldon. N.W. corner of churchyard.
Small, weatherboarded, iron grille in door.

GLOUCESTERSHIRE

POUNDS

AMPNEY S. PETER. 3 miles E of Cirencester. E of lane leading to old school. GR 082013.
Rectangular. Drystone walls S and W. N and E walls formed by Pound Cottage. Used as garden.

BIBURY. N side of A433 in village.
Large rectangle. Drystone, vertical coping. E wall remains to 10′ and few courses of W wall. Contains public conveniences.

CHARFIELD. 2 miles N of Wickwar. Next to bungalow approaching old school. GR 717914.
About square. Rubble, with vertical coping. Entrance broken down to admit car. Condition otherwise good (1974).

CRANHAM. 5 miles N.E. of Stroud. In village. GR 897130.
Squarish. Tall drystone walls with verticals as coping. Good oak gate. Needs some repair (1974).

DIDMARTON. 5 miles S.W. of Tetbury. N.W. side of A433.
Square. Drystone, with front corners nicely rounded. Most of front wall missing, remaining walls decaying. Contains locked shed. Used by Council.

DONNINGTON. W of A429, 2 miles N of Stow on the Wold. Adjacent to Weasel Farm, which provides S wall.
Nearly square. Drystone, vertical coping. Good, except part of N wall fallen (1974). Used as garden and car standing.

LONGNEY. 6 miles S.W. of Gloucester. Immediately S of Church.
Square. Brick, with semicircular blue brick coping. Buttressed. Old wooden gate. Very good except for one crack.

MINCHINHAMPTON. Old Common. GR 876011.
Rectangular. Drystone coursed, with flat coping. Iron gate.

NEWNHAM. 11 miles S.W. of Gloucester. At road junction W of A48.
Rectangular. Coursed stone with semicircular coping. Iron gate. In use to about 1920. Needs some repair (1975).

PAINSWICK. N end of town. W of B4073. GR 866107.
Large square. Drystone up to 5′ with remains of coping. E wall removed. Used as car standing.

PARK END. FOREST OF DEAN. By the Pike (Turnpike House).
Rectangular. Pointed split oak palisade, wide gate similar. Opposite end roofed and contains manger. Divided into two by oak posts, pig wire and small gate. Carefully maintained, and liable for use.

RANGEWORTHY. GR 6886. N end of village, E side of B4058, opposite Pool Farm.
Square. Rubble, partly drystone. Walls now about 3′, cement-capped, set with verticals with a raffish look. Floored with concrete slabs, some coloured. Restoration well-meant, but in a manner which must have provided some fun.

Remains or site: Ampney Crucis, Aust, Arlingham, Brandrick's Green (Forest of Dean), Compton, Cold Ashton, Elkstone, Olveston, Over, S. Briavel's, Saul, Staunton on Wye, Tockington, Twyning.

Gloucestershire—cont.

LOCKUPS

IRON ACTON. GR 6783. In the N wall of the Church tower. Entrance within the Church, tall, very narrow, arched head. The cell is very small, with tiny slit window placed very high. Small recess on W wall, 2 iron brackets at different levels on E wall. Ancient wooden door. Altogether a puzzling structure.

MORETON IN MARSH. In the curfew tower. An old studded door, without light or grille. Interior inaccessible.

NORTHLEACH. Small cell, 8' square, adjacent to seventeenth century Post Office. Barrel vault, wooden door with grille. Contains a narrow bench.

WOTTON UNDER EDGE. In the cellar of the Tolsey, corner of High Street and Market Street. Not accessible.

HAMPSHIRE

POUNDS

NEW FOREST. 1. Near Stoney Cross. GR 257104.
 Rectangular. Post and rails. Two-way gate at W. Secondary division, gated, on E leads to narrow pen with gate at far end. Used during drifts for marking and tail-cutting by the agisters.

 2. Ladycross. N side of railway bridge. GR 334036.
 Nearly square. Posts and 5 stout rails to 5'. 5-barred gate. Small bay at N.W. without exit. Condition excellent. In use.

 Elsewhere in the forest are a large number of small square wooden pounds, all well maintained.

SOUTHAMPTON. Right side of main Hill Lane entrance to common.
 Square. Stout oak posts and two iron rails, with close narrow verticals in lower half. Well maintained, and fit for use.

Remains or site: New Forest (Rowbarrow), Binstead, Curdridge, Dibden, Greywell, Meon Stoke, Newnham, Tadley.

HEREFORDSHIRE

POUNDS

BROCKMANTON. 3 miles E of Leominster. GR 547594.
 Triangular enclosure, about ¼ acre, beside brook below Pound Farm, the brook forming one side. Five barred gate. (Identification probable, but not known to farmer).

BROMYARD. E of town, N side of A44 at GR 659544.
 Irregular quadrilateral. Stone, built into bank on W. Good stone entrance. Recently restored (1974).

CANON PYON. 7 miles N.W. of Hereford. Adjacent to Church. GR 451491.
 Square. Coursed rubble without coping. E wall deeply wind-furrowed. Some pointing needed (1974).

EWYAS HAROLD. 10 miles S.W. of Hereford. GR 3828. Dark Lane, adjacent to Alma Cottage.
 Long rectangle. Roughly coursed, with vertical coping. Altered: wide entrance with door, corrugated iron roof, used as store. Moved from lane S.E. of Church in 1859.

MARDEN. 5 miles N of Hereford. GR 522478. Adjacent to forge, and used as store.
 Squarish, with walls originally 7½' raised, and roofed. Wide entrance with wooden door not original. Fulfilling a useful function.

Herefordshire—cont.

Remains: Eardisley, Linton (GR 661252 – very tall wall on hillside), Upton Crews.

LOCKUPS

BRIDSTOW. 1 mile W of Ross on Wye. Adjacent to the White Lion.
Front room or rooms of upper storey of ancient sandstone house, converted by barring 3 mullioned windows, 2 on front, 1 in gable. No access.

PEMBRIDGE. A44 between Kington and Leominster. In roof of Market Cross, access by ladder. A wooden chamber about 10′ square. Small entrance, no door.

HERTFORDSHIRE

LOCKUPS

ANSTEY. (C). One bay of a mediaeval lychgate. Converted to a lockup with red brick walls.

BARLEY, (C). B1368, 4 miles S.E. of Royston, Cross Hill.
Square. Timber, vertical members, close set. Wooden door, with narrow vertical timbers. Pyramidal slate roof with pointed finial.

SHENLEY. (N.P). 6 miles S.E. of S. Albans. E of London Road, between the Queen Adelaide and Pound Lane.
Circular. Brick, plastered. Pointed door, and small barred windows with the inscription: Be sober – Do well – Fear not – Be vigilant. Eighteenth century, repaired 1810.

HUNTINGDONSHIRE

POUND

ELTON. 5 miles N.E. Oundle. At Over End.
Small square enclosure against wall of house. Wooden posts, iron rail and wire. Small wooden gate. Quite a toy pound.

Remains or site: Alconbury Weston, Ellington, Lower Benefield, Ramsey, Yaxley.

LOCKUPS

BROUGHTON. W of A141, 5 miles N.E. of Huntingdon. E of Church.
Square. Brick, gabled tiled roof. Domestic-looking wooden door with wooden lintel. Back wall has two very small openings, grilled, upper with bars vertical, lower horizontal.

EATON SOCON. A1, 1 mile S.W. of S. Neot's. S of Church.
Rectangular. Brick, gabled tiled roof. Pointed arch entrance in W wall, studded door, wooden frame with iron coat, grille below arch. In S wall 3 tiny semicircular apertures cut out of bricks. Plaque: The Eaton Socon Cage / This ancient lockup was built / in 1826 for the confinement / of local malefactors. / Restored in 1963 it is now / in the care of the / Bedfordshire and Huntingdonshire / Naturalists' Trust. Within: arched entrance to second chamber occupying S.E. corner. Door standing against wall.

FENSTANTON. N of A132, 4 miles S.E. of Huntingdon. Village centre.
Square. Brick. Has upper storey with clock on E face, and bell turret above. Pyramidal slate roof. Doors N and S, N one probably secondary. Flat brick arch to S one. Plain doors.

NEEDINGWORTH. B1085, 1 mile E of S. Ives. By War Memorial.
Rectangular. Brick. Dated 1838. Doorway has flat brick arch, wooden-framed. Lower part of door restored. Ancient massive pin hinges and fittings. Close iron grille. Single slope roof. Vaulted within. Bench opposite door. Plaque: Needingworth lockup. The parish constable kept criminals here while arranging for transfer to County Gaol for trial.

ISLE OF WIGHT

POUND

FRESHWATER. (C). Pound Green.
    Circular. Rubble with pebble top. Privately cared for, and used as garden.

KENT

POUND

TUNBRIDGE WELLS. Halfway up Grove Hill Road on left.
    Rectangular. Brick, with hipped slate roof. Later brick wall applied to front (road) side, short of roof. Replaces post and rails? Pound contains a manger.

Remains or site: Cowden, Dartford, Gillingham, Knockholt, Rainham, Wilsley, Ash Farm Smardon.

LANCASHIRE

POUNDS

ARKHOLME. B6254, 10 miles N.E. of Lancaster. By Church.
    Irregular quadrilateral. Coursed rubble, 5′ walls with flat coping. Entrance restored – turreted! Modern gate, with wire 'window'.

ELLEL. E of A6, 4 miles S of Lancaster. At Hampson Green, in garden of Ellel Bank.
    Circular, with 7′ stone walls. Good studded oak door to road, with stone lintel. An exceptionally good example. Sold to owner by the Parish Council.

FIELD BROUGHTON. (C). On A590, 2 miles N of Cartmel.
    Square. Rough stonebuilt. Restored 1971.

OUT RAWCLIFFE. N of A586, at Crook Gate, 6 miles S.W. of Garstang.
    Circular. 7½′ stone walls, roughly coursed. Stone entrance 3′ x 6′, with stone lintel. Back wall fallen for 8′ (1975).

SLYNE. A6, 3 miles N of Lancaster, opposite Cross Keys, with stocks.
    Horseshoe-shaped. Rubble, roughly coursed, with triangular stone coping, lost over a short length (1975). Contains stone trough.

WEST BRADFORD. 2 miles N of Clitheroe.
    Irregular shape, wall mostly curved. 5′ rubble wall with semicircular coping. Given to the village by Lord Clitheroe.

LEICESTERSHIRE

PINFOLDS

ANSTEY. B5327, 4 miles N.W. of Leicester. On the common.
    Horseshoe-shaped, with entrance at narrow end. Slatey stone wall to 7′, with brick entrance and coping.

BREEDON ON THE HILL. A453, 5 miles N.E. of Ashby de la Zouch. In village.
    Square. Random stone 7′ walls. Cage adjoining.

WYMESWOLD. B5324, 4 miles N.E. of Loughborough, W end of village.
    Rectangular. Posts (sleepers) and rails (split saplings). Approach closed either end with wide iron gate, and similar at far end of pinfold. Restored.

Site: Packington.

Leicestershire—cont.

LOCKUPS

BREEDON ON THE HILL. Part of complex with the pinfold.
> Circular. Coursed stone, with tall pointed roof, and ball finial. With the pinfold, this is a notable group.

PACKINGTON. (C). B5326, 2 miles S of Ashby. At crossroads N of village, site of pinfold adjoining.
> Hexagonal, sides and roof of brick, separated by a course of stone. Flat stone at apex, with small ball finial. No light. Oak door, with small perforated iron plate. Door nail-studded.

WORTHINGTON. 2 miles S of Breedon on the Hill. In village.
> Circular, with tall pointed roof. Coursed stone. Pinfold stood alongside until recent years.

LINCOLNSHIRE

PINFOLDS

EPWORTH. (1) A161, 8 miles N of Gainsborough. Rectory Street, nearly opposite the Old Rectory, birthplace of John Wesley.
> Large rectangle. Brick. S. wall decaying, but restoration imminent (1976). Building in N.E. corner may be a cage. (Below).

EPWORTH. (2) West End Road, S side.
> Almost rectangular. Brick, with 5' walls, narrow entrance. Contains mature ash tree (1974).

HECKINGTON. A17, 5 miles E of Sleaford. N side of street at W end of village.
> Square. 7' brick walls, internal corners rounded. Semicircular brick coping. 5' entrance with wooden gate. Some necessary repair has been done, and some paving put down.

RIPPINGALE. E of A15, 5 miles N of Bourn. Corner of Station Street and an estate lane.
> Rubble wall, 6' and very robust except for some defect in S.W. wall (1975). Entrance closed with sheet of corrugated iron.

WAINFLEET SAINT MARY. (C). 20 miles N.E. of Boston. On riverside, abutting on to Low Road.
> Octagonal. Walls 13' each side, 7' high. Hand-made brick. The opening consists of one side, into a field, closed by double doors. Now covered, with excellent slated roof. Privately owned, used as store. Needs some repair (1976).

Remains or site: Belton, Dunholme, Faldingworth, Ferriby, Hemswell, Marston, Stamford.

LOCKUPS

DIGBY. (N.P). and (C). 6 miles N of Sleaford. S.W. of Church.
> 'Like a pepperpot, hardly high enough to stand up in'. Coursed masonry, including dome with ball finial. Restored.

EPWORTH? Brick shed in corner of pinfold (1). Has low blocked opening in wall to road. Seems part of original structure.

LONDON

POUNDS

HAMPSTEAD. (C). Near Whitestone Pond, just below the highest point on Hampstead Heath.
> Circular. Brick, 7' walls. Wooden gate. Built 1787, to replace a pound removed by a man presented at the Manor Court. Side supports of gate formerly the jaw bone of a whale.

London—cont.

WIMBLEDON. (C). Near corner of Parkside Avenue and Parkside.
  Square. Post and rails, no gate. Restored.

MIDDLESEX

POUND

SOUTHGATE. (C). Half a mile S.E. of Southgate Underground Station along The Bourne,
  near The Woodman.
  Square. Post and rails. Carefully maintained. Last use 1904.

NORFOLK

POUNDS

DOCKING. (C). 6 miles S.W. of Burnham Market.
  Rectangular. Brick, with cage adjoining (Below). In the care of the Parish Council.
  Floored with shingle, and equipped with seat.

GIMINGHAM. (C). On crossroads, Mundesley to Southrepps, Trunch to Trimingham.
  Quadrangular. Flint, with brick corners and coping. Height 6–8'. Old wooden door
  and gateposts. Restored, and in the care of the Parish Council.

NORTH ELMHAM. (C). 5 miles N of East Dereham. On edge of old common in corner of
  enclosure road and Dereham – Holt Road.
  Square. Brick, with semicircular brick coping. Wide wooden gate.

Site: Sedgeford.

LOCK UPS

DOCKING. (C). Beside the pound.
  Rectangular. Flint with brick corners and pantiled roof. Barred opening at gabled end.

THETFORD. (N.P). In Cage Lane.
  Gabled, two bays, one with doorway, the other a big barred window.

NORTHAMPTONSHIRE

POUNDS

BRIXWORTH. A508, 7 miles N of Northampton. Junction of High Street and
  Northampton Road.
  Quadrangular. Bounded on N by 12' stone wall, elsewhere by low walls. Converted to
  garden, and carefully tended.

COTTINGHAM. N of A427, 8 miles N of Kettering. Blind Lane, opposite Pinfold House.
  Rectangular hedged area used as garden. The property of the Freeholders.

MIDDLETON. W of Cottingham. On the bend of School Hill.
  Large rectangle with 6' stone wall and vertical coping stones. Old entrance closed. New
  one from forecourt of adjoining house. Used as garden. The property of the
  Freeholders.

SULGRAVE. E of B4525, 7 miles N.E. of Banbury. Junction of road to Morton Pinkney
  and green lane to Weston, near Manor House.
  Quadrangular. Site cleared and planted as small garden with seat 1975.

Remains or site: Crick, Gayton, Milton Malsor.

Northamptonshire—cont.

LOCKUPS

GEDDINGTON. (C). A43, 4 miles N of Kettering. In the base of the Eleanor Cross.

GREAT WELDON. (N.P). A43, 8 miles N.E. of Kettering. On the green.
Circular, with conical roof. 'Probably eighteenth century'.

NORTHUMBERLAND

PINFOLDS

ALNWICK. (C). E end of Green Batt, top of Hotspur St. (Moved from elsewhere).
Circular. Large blocks of coursed sandstone, walls 6—8'. Gate.

ELSDON. (C). 9 miles S.W of Rothbury. GR9393. On green.
Circular. Large blocks, coursed. Very good example.

Remains or Site: Bedlington, Monkseaton, Newcastle (faces North Road — junior cricket
pitch for Royal Grammar School).

NOTTINGHAMSHIRE

PINFOLDS

BECKINGHAM. (C). 2 miles W of Gainsborough, A631.
Three sides formed by buildings, including the old Methodist chapel, the fourth a
brick wall.

EAST LEAKE. (C). 5 miles N.E. of Loughborough, on the green.
Square. Stone with coping. Walls raised with brick, and roofed with corrugated iron to
make garage.

EAST MARKHAM. (C). N of Tuxford. W side of Plantation Road, near junction with
Plantation Avenue.
Large rectangle. Stone, with internal corners rounded. Inserted into bank at rear.

GRASSTHORPE. (C). 4 miles S.E. of Tuxford, N side of village, 100 yards N of bridge, at
corner of Town Street and Copper Hill.
Square. Brick, walls 7', buttressed, the top 5 courses later, brick coping. Gateposts
stone-capped. 6' entrance with decrepit wooden gate. Inset stone commemorates the
Golden Jubilee 1897.

KIRKBY IN ASHFIELD. (C). 12 miles N.W. of Nottingham. Church Street, facing S.
Wilfred's.
Square. Large blocks of stone, with triangular stone capping. Walls 6'. Needs repair
(1975).

LAXTON. 3 miles S.W. of Tuxford, next to Dovecote Inn. Previously stood opposite the
inn.
Nearly square. Thinnish stone, with stone coping. Wide entrance, gated. Said to be
used occasionally.

NORWELL. (C). 6 miles N.W. of Newark. Bathley Lane, near Plough Inn.
Circular. Brick, entrance with brick pillars. Carefully restored, with some new brick,
and new gate.

SCARRINGTON. (C). 8 miles E of Nottingham. Main Street, by smithy.
Circular. Brick, English bond, walls 7', with saddleback brick coping. 7' entrance, with
wrought iron gate.

SCREVETON. (C). 3 miles N.E. of Bingham.
Circular. 7' brick wall, buttressed. Wooden gate.

Nottinghamshire—cont.

SCROOBY. (C). 2 miles S of Bawtry. Between churchyard wall and boundary of Brewster's (Pilgrim Father) Cottage.
Rectangular. Front wall roughly coursed, with irregular capping. Modern gate. Sign: The Village Pinfold.

SKEGBY. (C). 3 miles S.E. of Tuxford.
Quadrilateral. Rubble with capping. Said to be 18th century.

WOODBOROUGH. 7 miles N.E. of Nottingham. Main Street W of Church next Pinfold Close.
Square. Brick, with coping and wooden gate.

(Much of the above information is derived from the article entitled Village Pinfolds, in Heritage, Summer 1975, Nottinghamshire County Council).

OXFORDSHIRE

POUNDS

WEST ADDERBURY. 5 miles S of Banbury. GR 474357.
Rectangular. Coursed rubble, with nicely rounded S.W. corner and iron gate. Incorporated into garden of house.

BECKLEY. 5 miles N.E. of Oxford. Almost opposite inn.
Rectangular. 3' drystone walls, front wall lowered to 1' to display garden within. Site includes garage.

BOTLEY (N. HINKSEY, OXFORD). Field of about an acre, S side of A4141, 200 yards W of junction with A34. Registered common.

COMBE. (OXFORD). (C). Incorporated in the garden of Pound Cottage. Drystone walls.

FRITWELL. 5 miles N.W. of Bicester. GR 527295.
Large rectangle, now part of garden of bungalow. Good coursed rubble, N wall removed.

Remains or Site: Duns Tew, Ewelme, Murcott, Rollright, Steeple Aston, Sandford S. Martin.

LOCKUPS

BURFORD. Swan Lane, built on to Walnut Tree Cottage.
Square. Rubble, roofed with corrugated iron. The wall presented to the lane has two pairs of small circular openings, seemingly lined with clay piping. The opposite wall with entrance has been removed. Used as garden store.

WHEATLEY. 6 miles E of Oxford. W end of village, Littleworth Road.
Hexagonal pyramid on shallow plinth. Coursed rubble, walls 2' thick at base. Sides 7½'. Ball finial. Door original, 3 massive oak planks, with bolt. 1834.

RUTLAND

POUND

UPPINGHAM. S of Church. Large irregular quadrilateral, coursed blocks. S wall lowered, adjoining garden. Pound well maintained as garden. Notice reads: Pound overt or pinfold. The use of this dates back before 1634.

Remains: Caldecott.

SHROPSHIRE

POUNDS

HARLEY. 2 miles N.W. of Much Wenlock, off A458. GR 597014.
Squarish, 5' rubble walls. Entrance from road broken down. Repair urgent (1974).

KNOCKIN. 5 miles S.W. of Oswestry, B4398. N side of road at W end of village.
Irregular quadrilateral. Front of good sandstone blocks, smaller stone elsewhere.
Excavated into bank, and back wall has fallen (1975). Entrance in front wall has stone
sill.

LLANYBLODWELL. 5 miles S.W. of Oswestry. Main Llynelys-Llanrhaedr Road at
junction to village and church. GR 244230.
Squarish. Rubble. Property of Bradfords Estate, and receives some care, but needs
repair, and is being used as a dump (1975).

LOPPINGTON. 3 miles W of Wem, opposite the Church.
Rectangular. Large sandstone blocks.

MORVILLE. (C). A458, 4 miles W of Bridgnorth. Corner of car park of Acton Arms.
Rectangular. Random rubble. Restored.

RUDGE. 7 miles N.E. of Bridgnorth, near Rudge Hall GR 811975.
Circular. Sandstone with flag coping. Wide entrance.

WOLLERTON. 1 mile N.N.E. of Hodnet. S outskirts, E side of A53, on road junction.
Circular, with entrance in a flat face. Brick, with flag coping. Walls 6' with 3 shallow
buttresses, inside and outside. Wooden gate between brick piers. Restored.

Remains or site: Claverley, Donington, Ryton.

LOCKUP

BISHOPS CASTLE. In ground floor of Town Hall of about 1765. Two circular windows,
grated. Not accessible.

SOMERSET

POUNDS

BATHEASTON. A4, 3 miles E of Bath. Pound Hill, Northend, on R. ascending.
Irregular quadrilateral, rubble. Was probably moved from edge of common in 1814.
Was becoming derelict, with one wall fallen. Restored by The Batheaston Society
1973, grassed, and whitebeam planted.

BROMPTON REGIS. 4 miles N.E. of Dulverton. S.E. of Church, at entrance to Nicholls
Farm, adjacent to lockup. (Below).
Narrow rectangle, 6' stone walls, new gate at narrow end.

CARHAMPTON. 3 miles S.E. of Minehead. 300 yards S.E. of Church, on W corner of
junction of A39 and B3191.
About square. Random stone to 7'. Door in E wall. W wall formed by thatched
cottage. Used as garden.

CREECH S. MICHAEL. 3 miles E of Taunton. In Bull Street.
Large rectangle, random, wide entrance. Decaying (1973).

COMPTON MARTIN. 10 miles S.S.W. of Bristol. W side of A368, 100 yards N of Ring O'
Bells.
Narrow rectangle, rubble, original entrance from road. E wall almost completely
removed to join with garden. Used to about 1924.

CROSCOMBE. A37 between Wells and Shepton Mallet, fronting lane a few yards N of
Church tower.
Rectangular, drystone, roughly coursed. Walls taken down to a few courses except
N wall, which remains to 4'. Entrance has been carefully widened for use as car
stand.

CROWCOMBE. E of A358, 10 miles N.W. of Taunton. Opposite Church, abuts on mediaeval Church House.
Rectangular, rubble, with rough vertical coping. Brick arch over entrance. Wooden gate. A good example, carefully maintained.

DUNSTER. Lower end of town, 80 yards W of Foresters' Arms.
Rectangular, random stone, cement capped, modern gate, iron railings, spiked. Plaque: The old Dunster pound.

FIVEHEAD. S of A378 between Taunton and Langport. N of Baptist Chapel.
Square. Good coursed masonry to road, other walls random. Flag coping, slight iron gate. Restored by Womens' Institute as neat little garden.

HINTON CHARTERHOUSE. 6 miles S of Bath, E of B3110. Beside Church gate.
Long rectangle. Coursed rubble walls 7', S.E. corner nicely rounded. Narrow entrance with modern gate. Top of wall defective in parts, Used as wood store, and somewhat neglected (1975).

HUTTON. 2 miles S.E. of Weston super Mare. GR 3558. Church Lane at S.W. corner of Rectory garden.
Random walls 7' to 8'. Now incorporated in garden of Freshfields, with ornamental iron gate in W wall. Original entrance to road boarded up. Built 1872/3 to replace a pound the site of which is now part of entrance drive of School.

KEYNSHAM (1). B3316 on N.W. outskirts of Keynsham, on S.W. corner of crossroads at GR 644693.
Irregular quadrilateral. Low walls (one small section collapsed), except on E where wall is elevated above field and of good coursed masonry. Has been planted with shrubs but is now neglected (1974).

KINGSBURY EPISCOPI. 4 miles S of Langport. Corner of Orchard Lane, near lockup.
Random wall to 6'. Well-made entrance from lane, closed by flimsy modern door, but an ancient staple remains. Used as garden.

KINGSDON. 3 miles S.E. of Somerton. Pound at GR 517264.
Square. Well-built coursed rubble walls with vertical coping. Some recent pointing, but too much ivy (1973).

MUCHELNEY. 1 mile S of Langport. On corner S of Church. Small rectangular field, hedged, but wall to road has good entrance.

NORTH STOKE. E of A481, between Bath and Bristol. On corner opposite entrance to churchyard.
E wall complete, and lower courses of S and W walls. No N wall, ground sloping steeply from N and E. Well watered by streamlet which leaves through carefully made opening to drop about 2' to road drain.

NORTON S. PHILIP. A336 between Radstock and Trowbridge. W of Church at GR 773557.
Grassed rectangle 40 by 15 yards. Partly hedged, partly fairly recent post and rails. Good farm gate either end, into road and into field.

SHEPTON MALLET. E side of B3136 entering town from N.
Long rectangle, with long axis to road. Drystone wall to 6½', well-built entrance with single lintel stone shaped below to 4-centred arch. Some hinges remain. Back wall a steep cliff.

SOMERTON. W end of town. Road sign reads: Pound Pond.
Rectangular enclosure with iron gate.

TINTINHULL. E of A303, 3 miles S.W. of Ilchester. Church Street.
Long narrow triangle. Side next street bounded by massive stone posts (have been previously used) joined by chain. Remaining two sides are paths to Church, unfenced.

WEST BAGBOROUGH. W slope of Quantock 6 miles N.W. of Taunton. W of Rising Sun, on opposite side of road.
Square. Drystone wall 5'. W wall a barn. Slatted wooden gate. Overgrown (1977).

Somerset—cont.

Remains or site: Bathford, near Binegar (GR 606479), Compton Dando, Dulcote, Dunkerton, Gurney Slade, Keynsham (2), S. Catherine, Simonsbath, Watchet, Williton, Withypool.

LOCKUPS

BATHFORD. Off A4, 3 miles E of Bath. S side of Bathford Hill.
Square, 15'. Coursed rubble. Gable rises to 12'. Roof pantiled. Two cells, each 12' by 6', very well vaulted. Each has a stone structure about 2' high across one corner, now covered with a slab, but said to be a urinal. Wooden beds have been removed. W wall of W cell has a very narrow light with two bars. Original doors, studded, with original fittings and grilles.

CASTLE CARY. On Bailey Hill.
Circular. Coursed ashlar, including dome surmounted by boss. Ancient door up steps. Two small grilles in lower part of roof. 1779. Given to parish by lord of manor 1922.

KELSTON. E side of A431, S of the Crown. Roadside, flanked by wall.
Rectangular, coursed stone, pitched roof with stone tiles (ivy-covered 1976). Narrow entrance, old oak door, with grille, bars horizontal; hasp and padlock. Area to N probably site of the pound, long derelict.

KILMERSDON. GR 6952. B3139 near Church.
Square. Roughly coursed. Pyramidal stone-tiled roof, with boss finial. Pointed arched doorway with shaped voussoirs. Barrel vault. Used as bus shelter.

KINGSBURY EPISCOPI. GR 4321. In Street.
Octagonal. Well built of ashlar with pyramidal stone roof and boss. Interior drain in one angle looks original. Tiny slit window second side from doorway either way. Plain stone doorway. Original oak door has had some repair. No grille.

MELLS. GR 7249. In lane running S, W of Church.
Square. Pyramidal stone-tiled roof with flat circular top. Arched doorway, iron-framed. Original door on sill with original pin hinges, hasp and padlocked grille. Within, through a thick wall is a second ancient door.

MERRIOTT. E of A356. 3 miles N of Crewkerne. In Lower Street.
Rectangular. Stone roof, very well vaulted within. Plain stone doorway, grille above. Remains of old oak studded door, backed with iron.

MONKTON COMBE. 2 miles S.E. of Bath. In Mill Street.
Rectangular, with rectangular domed roof, no boss. All good ashlar. High in W wall are two sets of four ventilation holes. Square-headed doorway. 'Make believe' model door replacement with small grille. Metal plate with iron loop beside? function.

PENSFORD. GR 6263. E side of A37, next George and Dragon.
Octagonal, on plinth. Rubble wall, perfect stone dome with boss. Straight-headed doorway. Good oak door, probably not original, up steps.

SOMERTON. Attached to W gable end of 17th century Town Hall, contemporary.
Coursed stone, pantiled roof. Resembles a gabled porch, with good doorway (labels) and studded door. No light.

Remains: Brompton Regis, Batheaston (Grated window at rear of Poor House).

STAFFORDSHIRE

POUNDS

ILAM. 5 miles N.W. of Ashbourne. W side of road at GR 133520.
Rhomboidal. Drystone. Two entrances to field.

RUSHTON SPENCER. (C). 5 miles N.W. of Leek. Adjoins Royal Oak in centre of village.
Iron railings. 'Ideal as playground'.

Staffordshire—cont.

SALT. (C). 3½ miles N.E. of Stafford. Salt Banks Lane, off Sandon-Stafford Road, half a mile from village.
Square. Sandstone, with sandstone floor. Gate, trough and iron fodder rack lost during past 60 years.

WALTON-ON-THE-HILL. 3 miles S.E. of Stafford. E end of village.
Square. 7' brick walls. Roofed, and used as garage. Plaque: In former years/This building was/The village pound.

WATERFALL. (C). 7 miles S.E. of Leek.
Horseshoe shaped. Drystone, with vertical coping. Restored.

WEST BROMWICH. (C). GR 009925.
Elongated hexagon (53'). Brick walls, lower courses old brick, upper modern, height barely 3'. Interrupted by five 10' gaps, two in each long side, one opposite entrance, closed with two modern rails. No door. A puzzling structure.

Remains: Bagnall, Uttoxeter (Quadrangle of massive upright stones), Waterfall (2), in farmyard.

LOCKUPS

ALTON. (N.P). Near Old Coffee Tavern.
Circular, stone dome, 1819.

STAFFORD. (N.P). Next to White Lion, Lichfield Road.
Square. Stone. Vaulted inside.

SUFFOLK

POUNDS

BECCLES. 8 miles W of Lowestoft. On back road leading S towards common.
Circular. 8' brick walls, semicircular coping. New 5-barred gate. Many signs of old repair, but needs more, wall leaning out in places (1975).

BLUNDESTON. 3 miles N.W. of Lowestoft. Corner of Pound Lane, near E end of Church.
Circular. 8' brick walls, semicircular coping. Small wooden gate.

KEDINGTON. 2 miles N.E. of Haverhill. Attached to cottage called Bottle Hall.
Square, 6' brick walls 18" thick. Modern wide entrance.

WRENTHAM. 4 miles N of Southwold. Corner of B1127 and Priory Road.
Circular. Brick to 6' with triangular coping and rather nice pilasters. Slatted wooden gate. Needs some repair (1975).

Remains or site: Freckenham, Oulton, Somerleyton.

SURREY

POUNDS

ABINGER. 3 miles S.W. of Dorking. In garden of Abinger Manor Cottage, S.W. of Church.
Quadrilateral. Massive low stone walls, roughly coursed, semicircular coping.

BRAMLEY. 5 miles S of Guildford, beside the Church.
Squarish. Stone, with brick corners, front wall removed, seat within.

BROCKHAM. 2 miles E of Dorking. Just beyond the Duke's Head, near the common.
Square. Brick, with pillared entrance, closed by hurdle.

GODALMING. N of Church.
Irregular quadrilateral. Random walls; corners and entrances patched with brick. Coping: half vertical stones, half semicircular brick. Contains a mature tree. A stone set in the wall records: This stone marks the site of / the old Godalming rectory and / manor pound. Presented to the / borough by the Rev. M. J. Simmonds / Lord of the manor May 1933.

HAMBLEDON. 3 miles S of Godalming, in Hydestile Lane.
Roughly square. Random stone, brick corners. Plaque: The Old Pound / of the Manor / of Hambledon / Restored 1955.

HASCOMBE. 3 miles S. E. of Godalming.
Square. Random stone. No door.

LIMPSFIELD. 2 miles S. W. of Westerham. Hurst Green Road, on left just off A25.
Ten-sided, 8' very good random stone walls, with coping. Tenth side forms entrance. Plaque: Limpsfield Pound. An unusually ambitious example.

OXTED. 11 miles S. E. of Croydon, in Sandy Lane.
Rectangular. Random stone, brick corners. W side post-and-3 rails, with good wooden gate.

SHERE. 5 miles S. E. of Guildford, in Middle Street.
Rectangular. Random stone with brick corners and coping. Front wall removed. Seat provided, to make a neat little rest.

WESTCOTT. A25, 2 miles W of Dorking. N. W. corner of Westcott Green, Westcott Street.
Roughly square. Rubble with brick corners. Slatted door.

Remains or site: West Horsley.

LOCKUPS

LINGFIELD. (N.P). 3 miles N of East Grinstead. Plaistow Street, near Duck Pond. 'Cross and cage, a composite building, looking like an early Irish cell-church. The cage, built 1773, forms the "cell" '.

OXTED. (N.P). S side of High Street. The 'Old Lockup'. Above, a 17th century timber-framed house fronting on to Shorters Row.

SHERE. (N.P). Lower Street. 'Old Prison House. Seventeenth century half-timbering, with various fillings, including flint'.

SUSSEX

POUNDS

ISFIELD. (C). 5 miles N. E. of Lewes. Beside road 100 yards N of Isfield Mill.
Square. Brick with stone coping. Peephole in N side.

RUSTINGTON. 2 miles E of Littlehampton. N side of street, near Church, adjoining Pound Cottage.
Rectangular. Walls 5', coursed rounded flints.

SIDLESHAM. (C). B2145, 4 miles S of Chichester. Highleigh, at junction of 3 roads about a mile from Sidlesham Church.
Rectangular. Coursed flint walls 7' brick corners, and topped with flint chips. No door. Well restored, and now maintained by the Parish Council.

SLINDON. A29, 8 miles E of Chichester, on the top road near the old track leading to Duncton Beacon.
Square. Walls 6'. Coursed flint with brick course at half height and brick corners. Two walls capped with flint and mortar, two with brick.

WILMINGTON. (C). 4 miles N of Eastbourne. At Polegate, alongside the Priory.
Square. Flint, 5–6'. Parish Council proposing to carry out some repair (1974).

Sussex—cont.

Remains or site: Albourne, Amberley, Brighton (Cricketers' Hotel, Black Lion Street), Lavant, Winchelsea.

LOCKUPS

SADDLESCOMBE FARM. Near Poynings, 5 miles N.W. of Brighton.
Lean-to against barn. Rectangular. Flint with brick corners, and buttress on long side, slate roof, 3 tiny windows. A very ancient door, planks reinforced with old scythe blades. Elaborate fastening device. Known as the Poachers' Pound. A memorable survival.

SLINDON. Opposite the Rectory gate.
Rectangular. Flint, 7' to eaves, with brick doorway and coping. Gabled slate roof. Modern door. Oval light in gable.

WARWICKSHIRE

POUNDS

BARSTON. 8 miles W of Coventry. (1) In village street.
Squarish. One brick wall only remains. 'Landscaped' by Parish Council, and very neat.
(2) At Eastcote, on Hampton-Knowle Road.
Nearly square. Brick. Very full restoration by Parish Council in 1974, at cost of £500. New door made, copying the old, using the original hinges. A fine piece of conservation.

BENTLEY. 3 miles S. W. of Atherstone, W side of B4116.
Rectangular. Coursed sandstone 7', with remains of gates. Ivy-covered. Back wall fallen. Restoration quite possible, but in a remote spot.

BERKSWELL. 5 miles W of Coventry. Right side of road about 500 yards E of Church near crest of hill.
Rectangular. Squared red sandstone, paved with random sandstone. New wooden gate. Very well restored.

CLIFFORD CHAMBERS. 2 miles S of Stratford, W side of A46, opposite village, beside the old road.
Square. Brick, with triangular brick coping. 6' entrance. Well repointed, defective right side of entrance repaired, and three dead elms removed, through the initiative of the Parish Council 1977.

LONG COMPTON. A34, 4 miles N of Chipping Norton. (1) Belongs to thatched cottage W of A34.
Large rectangle. Drystone walls, modern iron gate. Needs some repair (1975). Sold by Parish Council.

NORTHFIELD. 5 miles S of centre of Birmingham. W side of road near Church, next to Great Stone Inn.
Square. Bounded by buildings except W side to road. Coursed red sandstone, large blocks. Arched entrance to an obtuse angle, followed in walling and coping. Modern iron gate. On either side an arched barred opening. A remarkable pound.

Remains or site: Long Compton (2) Radford Semele.

LOCKUPS

ALCESTER. A very small square brick cell in basement of 17th century Town Hall. Ancient door, with lock, heavily barred. Small grating above

WARWICK. Shire Hall, side facing Barrack Street.
A heavy, studded oak door, with grille, and original hinges, two bolts and padlocks. A second grille above, the width of the door-frame. Plaque: The original outer door of a prisoners' cell formerly within the County Gaol rebuilt on this site 1695 (following destruction of the original building by fire in 1694) and remaining in use until 1861. Pevsner states that the cell is an octagonal vaulted room, deep in the ground.

WESTMORLAND

Remains of a pinfold at Raisbeck, 2 miles E.S.E. of Orton.

WILTSHIRE

POUNDS

BIDDESTONE. 4 miles E of Chippenham.
    Large rectangle with good 7' walls. Contains Public Convenience.

BOX. 5 miles N.E. of Bath. On A4 E of lockup.
    Rectangular. Present entrance up steps. N wall the gable end of 17th century barn, W wall an old house. In care of the Parish Council. Paved and planted.

CALNE. N.E. side of A4 a short distance S.E. of Talbot Inn.
    Rectangular area. Two stone walls remain, being boundaries of a garden.

SEMLEY. 4 miles N.E. of Shaftesbury. E of Church, adjoins house.
    Square. 6' rough ashlar walls.

Remains or sites: Corsham, Lacock, Trowbridge (2).

LOCK UPS

BOX. W side of A4 at entrance to village from S.
    Square. Large blocks, domed roof set back above rather elegant cornice. Arched doorway with worn step. Small barred window on N Chimney at N.E. corner. Presented to the Parish Council by Courage (brewers) 1978.

BRADFORD ON AVON. On the town bridge, built out over a pier.
    Square. Probably originally a mediaeval chapel. Fine curved pyramidal roof with elaborate finial and weathercock with vane in form of a fish. Small grilled lights. Chimney in S.E. wall. Ancient oak nail-studded door with iron sill at height of 3'. Contains two compartments with iron bedsteads.

BROMHAM. W of A342, 3 miles N.W. of Devizes. N.E. corner of churchyard.
    Rectangular. Timber on brick, closed with horizontal timbers. Pyramidal stone-tiled roof, slobbered with cement. Secondary door into churchyard. Ancient door, restored below, and old lock. Restored 1978.

CASTLE COMBE. E of Market Cross, at rear of cottage next to inn.
    8' square lean-to. Good walling of large blocks. Vaulted. Sloping roof of massive stone tiles. Plain doorway; door has been removed. Used for drunks up to 1965.

CHIPPENHAM. The Old Yelde Hall. Down stone steps from the fifteenth century Hall.
    A windowless cell, now about 9' square, but originally twice this size, below the Council Chamber. Flat arch stone doorway, ancient studded double door. Timber ceiling.

HEYTESBURY. A36, 4 miles S.E. of Warminster. Set into wall in village street.
    Hexagonal, on plinth. Coursed stone, large blocks. Conical slate roof, with boss. Square-headed doorway. Original nail-studded door, with padlock. Small grille above.

HILPERTON. A361, 1 mile N.E. of Trowbridge. Built into wall outside Hilperton House.
    Octagonal. Walls and a fine dome of large blocks, boss finial. Original doorway walled up. Entrance from garden? Grant of £500 for restoration 1976.

LACOCK. A350, 4 miles S of Chippenham. East Street, adjacent to old barn.
    Square. Good coursed masonry with stone domed roof. Two pilasters on W wall. Ancient studded door beside S wall leads into passage closed at far end by wall, part of original structure. Large iron hinge in wall of entrance passage denotes entrance to lockup.

LUCKINGTON. B4040, 10 miles W of Malmesbury. Bristol Road.
    Rectangular. Massive stone blocks. Gabled roof smeared over with concrete. Old wooden door with hinged perforated iron plate. No other light or ventilation. Grant of £500 for restoration 1976.

SHREWTON. A344, 4 miles W of Stonehenge. By roadside in village. Has been moved for road widening and carefully rebuilt.
Circular. Coursed sandstone, large blocks, including dome. Boss finial. Ancient oak door. Small barred window.

STEEPLE ASHTON. 5 miles S of Trowbridge. On green.
Octagonal. Large blocks with domed stone roof and boss. Door with grille probably original.

TROWBRIDGE. N of bridge.
Square. Good coursed stone, cornice, pyramidal roof with boss. Two tiny rectangular lights to S. Porch on N, down steps. Has 2 cells. Plaque: A lockup circa 1758, used as such until the erection of the first police station in Trowbridge in 1854. Roof stripped off in a riot 1826 and prisoners rescued. In 1942 blast from a German bomb caused roof to collapse. Restored in 1950. Stocks existed alongside until mid 19th century.

WARMINSTER. N end of town in garage yard.
Rubble walls, tiled domed roof with boss. Has been much altered, and shape is now irregular, with jutting corner. Door modern.

The lockups of Wiltshire, appropriately known as 'blind houses', and believed to be about 200 years old, are a remarkable set. They are mostly in the west of the county, and the lockups of Somerset are very alike. Wiltshire County Council has published an informative leaflet on the lockups.

WORCESTERSHIRE

POUNDS

CHURCHILL. 3½ miles N.E. of Kidderminster, E of crossroads, ½ mile N.E. of Church. GR 884797.
Square. Brick. Plaque: Churchill village / pound / erected 1862 / renovated 1966.

FECKENHAM. 4½ miles S.W. of Redditch. S of Church.
Largish rectangle, 7 of 12 oak posts, and about half the rails carefully renewed in the not distant past. Condition exceptionally good for wooden pound.

MALVERN (GREAT). Cowleigh Road opposite Holy Trinity Church.
Square. Stout random walling to 6', with brick corners. Wooden door padlocked. Ivy-covered, but cared for (1975). Stocks and whipping post alongside. A notable group.

PERSHORE. S side of A44, W of town.
A replica built in 1977 of a pound which was quite derelict. Rectangular, 3 posts and rails, split logs. Rails slide at entrance.

LOCKUP

EVESHAM. The lockup was in a corner of the Town Hall. Dismantled in 1956, the ancient door, window grille, handcuffs and iron bed are displayed in the Almonry Museum.

HALESOWEN. Was behind 18–20 Church Street. Taken down during complete redevelopment. Rescued by Halesowen History Group, stones numbered and put aside. It is hoped that it will be taken over and re-erected at the Black Country Museum, Tipton Road, Dudley. Stone walls were raised with brick. Old grilled door.

YORKSHIRE

PINFOLDS

APPLETON LE MOOR. (C). N of A170, 6 miles N.W. of Pickering. End of village, near chapel, opposite council houses.
Rectangular. Drystone, uncoursed. Gate. Fairly sound, but filled with scrub. (1975).

BARKISLAND. (C). In grounds of old workhouse at Heald Wall Nook. GR 053202.
Circular. Drystone. Two stone posts at entrance. A stone channel through the wall allows water to be poured in.

Yorkshire—cont.

BIRSTWITH. 6 miles N.W. of Harrogate, road junction at Swincliffe Side.
Oval. Coursed stone, with coping. Entrance formed of massive blocks. One hinge of door remains. Becoming overgrown (1973).

BUCKDEN. B6160 at GR 9477. On village green.
Large quadrangular enclosure. Stone walls, small gate. Has been used as garden, now neglected (1975).

CARPERBY. A684, 5 miles W of Leyburn. S side of road in village.
Irregular narrow quadrilateral. Good walls, triangular coping. Small wooden gate.

DRINGHOUSES. A64, 2 miles S of York.
Square. Walls 5', good mellowed brick, with cement capping. No gate. Fine bronze plaque, letters filled with enamel: This Pinfold or Pound was originally an enclosure / in which straying cattle were confined pending the / payment of a fine. These structures were principally in / use in the 17th, 18th, and 19th centuries and were / generally situated on roadsides and areas of common / grazing.

EAST AYTON. (C). A170, 4 miles S.W. of Scarborough.
Irregular shape. Coursed stone to about 6', vertical coping, no gate. Needs some attention (1975).

EAST WITTON. (C). Middleham Road (A6105), just short of right turn into village.
Largish rectangle. No entrance from road. Two gates into fields.

FISHLAKE. W of A614, 8 miles N.E. of Doncaster. Next Sion Chapel.
Squarish, and quite large. Brick 5½'. Wooden gate fallen. Walls decaying. Could be restored (1973).

FOLLIFOOT. (C). A661, 3 miles S.E of Harrogate. Upper end of village.
Circular. 7 courses of stone, vertical stone coping. Height 6'. Wooden door. Part of manor of Rudding Park, kept in repair by Parish Council. Restored by public subscription for European Architectural Heritage Year 1975.

HEPTONSTALL. (C). 1 mile W of Hebden Bridge. Below Methodist Church adjoining village car park.
Square. Drystone.

HUDDERSFIELD. (C). Rectangular. Drystone. Entrance has lintel. Restored by the Civic Society.

HUNMANBY. (C). 3 miles S.W. of Filey.
About square. Coursed rubble with flat stone coping. Joined by a wall to the lockup. Inscribed stone reads: Village pinfold for impounding stray cattle. The owners claiming the cattle were required to pay a fine to the parish. Village jail 1834 for men and women delinquents. Needed chiefly at the Martinmas Hirings and Fair. (Below).

HUTTONS AMBO. (C). E of A64, 5 miles S.W. of Malton. Adjoins Manor Farm.
Nearly rectangular. Stone. Walls 5½'. No gate.

HUTTON BUSCEL. (C). A170, 6 miles S.W. of Scarborough. Edge of village in Great Moor Road.
Circular, 6½' walls, good coursed stone with semicircular coping. Overgrown (1975).

HUTTON-LE-HOLE. (C). 8 miles N.W. of Pickering. On edge of village.
Circular. Drystone, with vertical coping. Walls 4–5'. One wooden gatepost. Full of nettles (1974). In manor of Spaunton, whose Courts Leet and Baron still meet, and the pinder is still appointed.

ILKLEY. (C). Weston Road.
Rectangular. Walls 7½'. Coursed gritstone, semicircular capping. Gateway 4½', with large stone gate stops. Front wall removed.

MICKLEY. W of A6108, 5 miles N.W. of Ripon.
Squarish. Rubble walls. Modern iron gate. Belongs to Court Leet. Used as garden by Little Orchard (opposite).

Yorkshire—cont.

MIDGLEY. (C). A646, 4 miles W of Halifax. Cliff Hill Hall, pack horse track to Clay Pits. Left of lane, about 200 yards from village street.
Circular. Drystone walls.

NORTON (Doncaster). (C). Junction of High Street and Common Lane.
Large rectangle. Stone wall only 3'. Narrow pedestrian entrance, main gate locked. A children's playground.

RASKELF. W of A19, 2 miles N.W. of Easingwold. Road junction to Easingwold.
Octagonal. 10' brick walls, castellated. Pointed doorway, arched barred window either side. Iron gate. Looks 18th century. Unique design, quite Gothick!

REDMIRE. 4 miles W of Leyburn. In village.
Rectangular. Rubble walls, with boulders, to 7'. Wooden door. N.W. wall beginning to fall (1975).

RISHWORTH. (C). 6 miles S.W. of Halifax. On Long Causeway, Rishworth side of Head Bridge at Parrock Nook.
Square, 40'. Drystone walls 6½'. Two stone posts at entrance.

SEDBERGH. Roadside by Pinfold Caravan Site.
Circular. Random walling, much of it water-worn. Top cemented, and unorthodox 'rockery' coping. Two opposed entrances, E one with deep step. No doors. Carefully restored.

SNAINTON. (C). A170 between Pickering and Scarborough. Next to Fire Station.
Rectangular. Good stone walling with some vertical coping. Structurally sound, but overgrown with ivy (1974).

SPAUNTON. (C). 8 miles N.W. of Pickering.
Rectangular, on sloping ground. Drystone, shallow courses, with vertical coping. Walls 4½–6'. Restored.

SPENNITHORNE. (C). 2 miles E of Leyburn.
Large irregular quadrilateral, traversed by stream. Good stone walls.

SPOFFORTH. A661 between Harrogate and Wetherby. Opposite Memorial Hall.
Rectangular. Good coursed walls 3'. Front wall looks recent. Now the forecourt to two cottages.

STAVELEY. 4 miles S.W. of Boroughbridge. At entrance to village from E.
Circular. Random stone, with stone coping.

STOKESLEY. (C). A172. 8 miles S of Middlesborough. Opposite New Inn.
Square. Brick. 4' walls, with stone coping. Repaired by Stokesley Society and metal plaque placed. In private ownership.

SWAINBY. (C). A172, 10 miles N.E. of Northallerton. In village street.
Rectangular. Massive stone blocks with semicircular coping. Restored and converted to garden 1975.

THRESHFIELD. B6265/B6160, 1 mile W of Grassington. Opposite manor and green.
Irregular rectangle, long side 13 yards. Short stretch of wall opposite entrance fallen. Masonry otherwise good (1975).

TICKHILL. (C). A631/A60, 6 miles S of Doncaster. Junction of Pinfold Lane and Rawson Road, W of Church.
Limestone. Small house attached. Conveyed from Duchy of Lancaster to Tickhill UDC 1921. Used in living memory. Restored as garden and small shrubbery 1977.

TONG. (C). 4 miles S.E. of Bradford. Corner of Keeper Lane and Tong Lane.
Oval. Random stone with capping. Flanked by village pump and old wheelwright's shop. Restored.

WARLEY (Halifax) (C). Near Sentry Edge, Mount Tabor. Stock lane, opposite Mare Hill Farm.
Circular. Drystone, 7'. Two stone gateposts.

Yorkshire—cont.

Remains or site: Appleton Roebuck, Beal, Burn, Hampsthwaite, Heck, Higham, Malham, Newton upon Rawcliffe, Norland, Pecket Well, Rawcliffe, Southowram, Stainland, Sykehouse.

The Metropolitan Borough of Calderdale supplied a helpful list of pinfolds in its area.

LOCKUPS

HUNMANBY. (C). (See under pinfold).
Rectangular. Brick, with hipped slate roof. Two cells, two doors, with grille over each.

HOLME UPON SPALDING MOOR. (N.P). 20 miles W of Beverley. Workhouse Farm, Howden Road.
Circular.

ILLINGWORTH. (N.P). 2 miles N.W. of Halifax. Keighley Road by the churchyard.
Arched doorway and circular windows. 1823. Inscribed: Let him that stole steal no more but rather let him labour working with his hands the thing which is good that he may give to him that needeth.

Fig. 11 : Park Pike, [Forest of Dean], Glos.

GLOSSARY

ATTACH — Seize by lawful authority.

COURT LEET — Court dealing with the business of a manor; not the lord's business, which came under the Court Baron.

CUSTODIA LEGIS — Legal custody.

DAMAGE FEASANT — Doing damage (usually of trespassing cattle).

DISTRAINT, DISTRESS — Seizure of property to enforce payment.

HAINING, HEYNING — Enclosing for cattle, often temporarily.

HOMAGE — All the tenants of a manor.

HUNDRED — A division of a shire.

LATHE — Administrative district of Kent.

IN MERCY — Liable to punishment.

RAPE — Administrative division of Sussex.

REEVE — Manorial officer, representing the tenants.

REPLEVIN — Restoration of distrained goods on pledge of submission to trial.

STINTED — Limited, pro rata.

TENTH AND FIFTEENTH — A tax on movables, the former in towns, the latter elsewhere.

WAPENTAKE — Division of a shire in eastern England.

REFERENCES

1. Maine, Sir Henry. Early History of Institutions. 1875. p.263.

2. Ibid. p.261.

3. Greenwell, W. Ed. Surtees Society 1852. Vol 25. Bolden Buke.

4. Grundy, G.B. Wiltshire Archaeological Magazine 1939, Vol 42, p.560.

5. Halsbury's Statutes of England 3rd edition 1971, Vol 9, p.504.

6. Ibid. p.507.

7. Ibid. p.510.

8. Cornish Archaeology 1964 Part 3, p.5.

9. Peterborough Manor Court Roll. Personal communication.

10. Greenwell, W. Bolden Buke. Loc. cit.

11. Greenwell, W. Ed. Surtees Society 1857. Vol. 32. Bishop Hatfield's Survey.

12. Barrett, F.T. West Sussex Gazette, 8 April 1965.

13. Personal communication.

14. Amphlett, J. Ed. Worcestershire Historical Society 1910. Court Rolls of the Manor of Hales.

15. Ratcliff, S.C. and Johnson, H. C. Eds Warwick County Records. Quarter Sessions Records. Indictment Book 1941.

16. Cunnington, B.H. Records of Wiltshire 1932. Wiltshire Quarter Sessions of the seventeenth century.

17. Ratcliff, S.C. and Johnson H.C. Loc. cit.

18. Thomson, W.S. Ed. Lincolnshire Record Society 1944, Vol. 36, pp. 4/5. A Lincolnshire Assize Roll for 1298.

19. Ilkley Manor Court Roll. Personal communication.

20. Burne, S. A. H. Ed. Staffordshire County Council 1931. Quarter Session Rolls. p. 115.

21. Hearnshaw, F. J. C. Ed. Southampton Court Leet Records 1905, p.278.

22. Ibid. p.355.

23. Marsh, A. E. W. 1903. History of the Borough and Town of Calne.

24. Wiltshire Archaeological Magazine 1930. Vol 45, p.84.

25. Whitty, R. G. H. Wiltshire Archaeological and Natural History Society Records Branch 1934 Wiltshire Quarter Sessions and Assizes 1736, Vol 11, p.275.

26. Mabbs, A. W. Ed. 1953. Calne Guild Stewards' Book 1561–1688.

27. Bennett. H. S. 1937. Life on the English Manor p.195.

28. Farr, M. W. Wiltshire Archaeological and Natural History Society Records Branch 1959 Vol. 14, p.190.

29. Grinsell L. V. et al. 1950. History of Swindon p.70.

30. Manley, F. H. Wiltshire Archaeological Magazine 1927/9, Vol 44, p.429 et seq.

31. Hertfordshire County Council. Hertfordshire Quarter Sessions Vol. 5.

32. Whitty, R. G. H. 1934. The Court of Taunton in the sixteenth and seventeenth centuries p.86.

33. Oxford Record Society. Vol. 40, pp. 106/7. Bye-Laws of the Manor of Islip.

34. Peterborough Manor Court Roll. Personal communication.

35. Langton Matravers Manor Court Roll. Personal communication.

36. Ratcliff, S. C. and Johnson, H. C. Loc. cit.

37. Oxford Record Society Vol. 41 Henley Borough Records Assembly Books p.34.

38. Mabbs. A. W. Loc. cit.

39. Personal communication.

40. Victoria County History of Somerset. 1974. Vol 3 p.16.

41. Somerset Records Society 1890, Vol 4, p.16.

42. Cruse, E. J. 1965. Castle Combe.

43. Personal communication.

44. Personal communication.

45. Hearnshaw, F. J. C. Loc. cit.

46. Coke, Sir Edward 1644 Fourth Part of the Institutes of the Laws of England.

47. Victoria County History of Wiltshire 1959 Vol. 4, p. 429.

48. Hart, C. E. 1951 Commoners of Dean Forest.

50. Dartmoor Preservation Association 1890 (Private publication) Short History of the Rights of Common upon the Forest of Dartmoor and the Commons of Devon p.15.

50. Ibid. p.54.

51. Ibid. p.70.

52. Personal communication.

53. Mac Dermot, E. T. Revised Edition 1973. The History of the Forest of Exmoor.

54. Notes and Queries 1888 Series 7 Vol 16 p. 408.

55. Dartford Chronicle 19 December 1969.

56. Sweetman, G 1903 History of Wincanton p. 190.

57. Morris, W. 1885 Swindon p. 465.

58. Mabbs, A. W. Loc, cit.

59. Chamberlain, J. A. 1976 Chippenham.

INDEX

Fig. 12 : Orsett, Essex

Fig. 13 : Hunmanby, Yorks. [Pinfold and lockup]

14th. Century Inn and Pound, Waltham-St-Lawrence.

ig. 14 : Waltham St. Lawrence, Berkshire

ig. 15 : Tunbridge Wells. [A rare roofed building]

57

Fig. 16 : Raskelf, Yorkshire

Fig. 17 : Pangbourne, Berks.

Fig. 18 : Bradford-on-Avon, Wilts.

[In Kenneth Grahame's garden]

Fig. 19 : Batheaston, Somerset [now Avon] [Restoration]

Fig. 20 : Spital Pinfold, Lower Bebington, Cheshire

Fig. 21 : Blundeston, Suffolk

Fig. 22 : GOING – Didmarton, Glos.

23 : GONE – East Stoke, Dorset

24 : A lorry passed by. Woodbury, Devon

Fig. 25 : Appleton le Moor, Yorkshire

Fig. 27 : Conversion to other use [bus shelter]. Hampsthwaite, Yorks

Fig. 26 : Wheatley, Oxon

63

Fig. 28 : Pound and lockup. Breedon on the Hill, Leics.

Fig. 29 : Restoration: rebuilding Batheaston 1973